D1168369

3 1160 00557 9466

Elizabeth Dole

Women in Politics

Madeleine Albright

Benazir Bhutto

Hillary Rodham Clinton

Elizabeth Dole

Nancy Pelosi

Queen Noor

WOMEN in POLITICS

Elizabeth Dole

Dale Anderson

CHELSEA HOUSE
PUBLISHERS
A Haights Cross Communications Company
Philadelphia

CHELSEA HOUSE PUBLISHERS

VP, New Product Development Sally Cheney
Director of Production Kim Shinners
Creative Manager Takeshi Takahashi
Manufacturing Manager Diann Grasse

Staff for ELIZABETH DOLE

Executive Editor Lee Marcott
Associate Editor Kate Sullivan
Production Editor Megan Emery
Photo Editor Sarah Bloom
Series & Cover Designer Terry Mallon
Layout 21st Century Publishing and Communications, Inc.

A Haights Cross Communications ⚹ Company

www.chelseahouse.com

First Printing

9 8 7 6 5 4 3 2 1

Library of Congress Cataloging-in-Publication Data

Anderson, Dale, 1953-
  Elizabeth Dole / Dale Anderson.
    v. cm. — (Women in politics)
  Includes bibliographical references and index.
    Contents: Senator Dole — Growing up in Salisbury, 1936-1954 — A remarkable
education, 1954-1965 — A young professional, 1966-1975 — Washington's power
couple, 1975-1987 — Labor secretary and Red Cross champion, 1987-1996 —
History maker, 1996-2003.
    ISBN 0-7910-7733-0 — ISBN 0-7910-7997-X (pbk.)
    1. Dole, Elizabeth Hanford—Juvenile literature. 2. Women cabinet officers—
United States—Biography—Juvenile literature. 3. Cabinet officers—United
States—Biography—Juvenile literature. 4. American Red Cross—Biography—
Juvenile literature. 5. Women legislators—United States—Biography—Juvenile
literature. 6. Legislators—United States—Biography—Juvenile literature. 7.
United States. Congress. Senate—Biography—Juvenile literature. [1. Dole,
Elizabeth Hanford. 2. Cabinet officers. 3. Legislators. 4. Women—Biography.] I.
Title. II. Series.
  E840.8.D63A53 2004
  328.73'092—dc22

                                                              2003025621

Table of Contents

Elizabeth Dole

Senator Dole

To achieve success is to find something that infuses you with a
sense of mission, with a passion for your life's work.
—Elizabeth Dole, *Business Woman Magazine*, 1999

On February 24, 2002, Elizabeth Hanford Dole came home to
Salisbury, North Carolina. She strode into the crowded gym of
Catawba College to announce that she was running for one of
North Carolina's two seats in the United States Senate. Some
3,000 people—including Dole's 101-year-old mother and her
husband, the former senator Bob Dole—filled the room, eager
to cheer for their hometown heroine.

In her speech, Dole outlined several themes that she would
stress throughout her Senate campaign. But hers was not a
typical campaign speech. Dole was coming home, and she
had some personal things to say. She thanked the hometown
crowd for their enthusiastic support. She also paid tribute to
her parents, who had taught her an important lesson as a

child: that "success is measured, not in material accumulations, but in service to others."[1]

These words sum up the career of Elizabeth Hanford Dole. For more than forty years, she has devoted herself to public service. As she wrote in her autobiography, "I tell youthful audiences they can find no higher calling in life than that of public service. They may not get rich, but they'll enrich the lives of others."[2] In speech after speech, she has repeated this message. In 1998, she told it to the graduates of Harvard University's Kennedy School of Government. In 2000, she delivered a similar message to graduates of the University of Cincinnati and Duke University. The way she explained it to the graduates of South Carolina's Erskine College best sums up her life story and her beliefs:

> As a young woman, looking forward to my life's work, I found my highest ideals in public service. I believed, and still believe, that the greatest life is a life of public service—and that public service, in a democracy such as ours, is one of the most satisfying ways to give [to others]."[3]

In 2002, Dole was poised to enter a new phase of public service. Though she had held many jobs in the government, all had come to her by appointments. In aiming for the Senate, she hoped to win an elective office for the first time in her life. If she won, she would make history. She would become the first woman elected to the U.S. Senate from North Carolina. But breaking barriers was familiar ground for Dole. When she entered public service in the 1960s and 1970s, government was still largely a man's world. She had to struggle against prejudice because many people believed that women could not be serious about government work or competent enough to do it. She had to face discrimination that prevented her from working effectively. There was a time, for instance, when she was stopped from attending a meeting because it was held in a club women were not permitted to enter.

Determined to succeed, Elizabeth Hanford Dole overcame these obstacles to build a solid career. She worked in a government office that protected the rights of consumers. She served as a commissioner on the Federal Trade Commission. This powerful agency makes sure that businesses operate fairly and legally. She held cabinet posts in the administrations of two different presidents and was the first woman to do so. She also served as president of the American Red Cross, one of the largest nonprofit institutions in the country.

Now she was running for the Senate. Her campaign got off to a difficult start. She had planned to launch it on September 11, 2001. That was the day, of course, that terrorists destroyed the Twin Towers of the World Trade Center and blew a gaping hole in the Pentagon, which houses the U.S. Department of Defense. Several thousand people died and more were injured. In the face of this atrocity, Dole postponed her announcement. In fact, she delayed entering the Senate campaign for several months. Finally, in February, she was ready to go.

To become a senator, Dole had to win two elections. First she had to beat other Republican candidates in a primary election in which only Republicans voted. If she won that vote, she would become the Republicans' official candidate for senator. Then, in November's general election, she would compete against the Democratic candidate.

Some important figures supported Dole's candidacy. President George W. Bush campaigned for her. Retiring conservative Senator Jesse Helms, who was very popular among North Carolina Republicans, also supported her.

Still, Dole came under some criticism. Other Republican

candidates complained that she refused to join them in debates. Her reason for that decision could be found in poll results. Surveys of voters during the campaign gave Dole a huge lead over her rivals. Not surprisingly, candidates with such large leads rarely debate their opponents, feeling that debating can only hurt them and help the other candidates. Some reporters criticized her as well. They said she was running a celebrity campaign. As one columnist put it, she had "a shell campaign—no debate, no issues, no substance."[4]

REPUBLICANS AND DEMOCRATS

The Republican Party and the Democratic Party are the two main political parties in the United States. All Republicans do not think alike, nor do all Democrats. Both parties include great numbers of people with a mix of political beliefs. Still, most people in each party do share certain values.

Republicans tend to be more conservative. They worry about the federal government becoming too large and too powerful and believe that local and state governments are best suited to handle many issues, such as education. They favor low taxes, believing that high taxes hurt businesses and workers. They tend to favor businesses, which they think provide the power to make the economy grow. They typically want fewer government controls on society, arguing that this gives people more freedom.

Democrats tend to be more liberal. They believe the government should protect people from powerful groups, such as major corporations, that would otherwise dominate American life. They also think the government should help people with disadvantages or those who suffer from discrimination and should support and protect the poor, members of minority groups, and women. While they do not want high taxes, they are willing to accept higher taxes to provide the money needed for government programs they think are important.

These attacks revived old complaints that Dole was all style and no substance, an allegation that was somewhat harsh. Dole did talk about issues in her speeches, and she often answered reporters' questions and strongly expressed her opinions. In the wake of the September 11 terrorist attacks, she wanted to make sure the nation had strong defense. She wanted to boost North Carolina's economy by helping farmers, owners of small businesses, and workers of all types. She wanted to improve education and protect the environment. She wanted to make health care easier to afford. Finally, she promoted public service and women's rights. As she told an interviewer, "I want to inspire young people that public service is a noble thing to do—and give women a place at the policy table." [5]

Still, she ran her campaign like the front-runner, avoiding debates so she could avoid mistakes. She ran a carefully planned and controlled campaign. She also remained charming despite the long hours and hard work.

One reporter described her careful preparation:

Elizabeth Dole gets ready for every event as if she's having tea with the Queen. . . . At a rally in a tobacco warehouse . . . Dole appears in a bubble-gum pink suit with beige pumps and stockings. If someone were to, say, spill barbecue on her, a mint green spare is hanging in her Buick sedan." [6]

Dole campaigned with a determination to succeed. She took nothing for granted and crisscrossed the state to reach every corner. She worked hard to raise the money that every political campaign needs to survive. Recognizing that some of her positions did not reflect the views of most North Carolina Republicans, she was flexible enough to modify some of those positions. In 1999, for instance, she had sharply criticized laws that allowed people to carry concealed handguns. But North

Carolina had such a law, and most state Republicans backed it. Dole dropped her opposition. She said that she had been convinced by arguments that states with concealed-gun laws saw the rates for certain crimes drop.

Her strategy paid off. She won the September primary election by an overwhelming majority, taking about 80 percent of all Republican votes. Facing her would be the winner of the Democratic primary, Erskine Bowles. Bowles had been a top advisor to President Bill Clinton, and like Dole, he had never held elective office.

Dole and Bowles fought a tough campaign. They spent about $21 millions between them, making it one of the most expensive Senate campaigns in history. In their two televised debates, they criticized one another for being out of touch with the people. Each ran tough ads criticizing the other candidate's stand on issues. Bowles claimed that one Dole ad criticized his wife, a charge Elizabeth Dole denied. Both appealed to important party leaders to appear on their behalf. President Bush— who was very popular in North Carolina—visited the state three times to support Dole.

Dole led in the polls early in the race, and she held that lead as the election neared. She worked hard, traveling to each one of the state's hundred counties. In a burst of activity during the last two weeks of the campaign, she logged about 2,000 miles, reaching out to people across the state. She also spent considerable time listening to the concerns of ordinary voters.

On election night, all the work paid off. On November 5, 2002, Elizabeth Dole won the Senate seat. She polled about 54 percent of the vote to Bowles's 45 percent. "We did it tonight," she told cheering supporters in Salisbury. "We made history."[7]

A few weeks later, Dole was back at her Washington home preparing to enter the Senate. A brief scare threatened to spoil her pleasure in the event. Early in January, her mother

As her husband, Senator Bob Dole, looks on, Elizabeth Dole is sworn in as the first woman to represent the state of North Carolina in the U.S. Senate on January 7, 2003. Although she had been a public servant since graduating from Harvard Law— including work as a public defender, White House cabinet member, and president of the American Red Cross—becoming a senator was a major milestone for Dole. It marked the first time she had been chosen by the people, not appointed by an individual.

felt ill and had to be taken to a hospital back in Salisbury. Fortunately, the problem appeared to be minor and she was released after a week.

Relieved that her mother was not seriously ill, Dole plunged ahead with her new life. On January 7, 2003, she took the oath of office along with ten other newly elected senators.

Elizabeth Dole's Senate campaign and victory revealed many things about her character. She has charm and personal appeal. She likes to plan and control her life. She has the determination to get what she wants, even if barriers stand in her way. She prefers working with others rather than fighting, but in a struggle she will act to win. Elizabeth Dole did not acquire these characteristics on the eve of her senatorial campaign—they developed well before, beginning with her youth in a small North Carolina town.

Growing Up in Salisbury

1936–1954

I'm a long way from Salisbury and the innocence of 1950s small-town America. However, we are the sum of our choices, and the experiences I had on the journey from Salisbury to Washington taught me invaluable lessons. The day you forget where you're from is the day you should leave public service.
— Elizabeth Dole, *Business Woman Magazine*, 1999

Elizabeth Dole's life was deeply influenced by her parents, her childhood, and her hometown. Born Elizabeth Hanford on July 29, 1936, she was the second—and last—child of John Hanford and Mary Ella Cathey Hanford.

Salisbury, where she grew up, is a small city in central North Carolina, lying between Charlotte and Winston-Salem. The city sits in the picturesque Piedmont section of North Carolina, a plateau region that rises up to the Blue Ridge

Mountains farther west. The area has lovely weather. The relatively high altitude cools the intense heat typical of the southern United States, making summers pleasant. Winters are mild, with highs around 50 degrees and little snow.

Salisbury and the surrounding area have a long history. Frontiersman Daniel Boone lived nearby for more than a decade. He left that home to begin his exploration and settlement of Kentucky. Settlers in Rowan County, where Salisbury stands, and a neighboring county protested British rule in 1775 and called for the British colonies to unite against a common enemy. Andrew Jackson studied law in Salisbury in the 1780s. During the Civil War, the town had a prison for captured Union soldiers. Thousands died there; their burial place—less than half a mile from Elizabeth Hanford's childhood home—is now a national cemetery.

A Cathey—a member of her mother's family—was among the first settlers of Rowan County back in British colonial times. Another Cathey ancestor had taken part in the 1775 protest against the British government. The Hanfords arrived in Salisbury in 1905 when John Hanford's parents left Colorado because his mother's health suffered from that state's high altitudes. They settled in Salisbury because the town had a reputation for good music, and both loved music. Elizabeth's grandfather also hoped to turn his hobby of growing flowers into a business there. The business flourished, and their son John took it over in 1914. In time, John also became the conductor of the town band.

Elizabeth Dole's parents met on a streetcar. When Mary Cathey got on the streetcar, she found the town band already on board. They were traveling, in uniform, to a concert. She was not much impressed by most of the band members, whose behavior struck her as immature. Their leader, young John Hanford, was different. "He sat there, very dignified, with his hands folded, and I thought he was very good looking," she told a journalist years later.[8] Apparently Hanford found her interesting as well. Cathey often practiced playing the organ at a local church—which happened to stand next door to Hanford's home. He frequently came outside so he could hear her playing through the church's open windows.

Over time, the two became romantically involved. Their relationship hit a bump in the road when Hanford took another girl to see a play and was almost ended by another obstacle. Mary Cathey was a talented musician. Her parents hoped that after high school she would study at the Juilliard School in New York City, one of the nation's foremost music schools. John Hanford worried that if she left Salisbury, she would leave his life. One day, he proposed to her and asked her to give up her music career. Mary Cathey agreed, and they were married.

They moved in with John Hanford's parents, and remained in this home even after the elder Hanfords died. It was there that their first child, John Junior, was born. Thirteen years later, so was Elizabeth. Three years after her birth, the family moved to a new house on South Fulton Street. In her memoir, Elizabeth Dole fondly remembers the huge magnolia tree in the front yard, the large entrance hall with its spiral staircase to the second floor, and the attic room she loved to sit in on rainy days. The brick and stucco home is still in the family, and Dole became its owner in 2001.

The Hanford home was comfortable, loving, and full of faith. John Hanford's flower wholesaling business remained successful even during the Depression. Thus, the family could afford to send their daughter to summer camps and pay for piano lessons. Even during those difficult years, the family could afford a college education for young John.

There can be no doubt that the family was a loving one. In her autobiography, Elizabeth Dole wrote that she could not "imagine a more loving environment to raise a child" than her parents' home.[9] She says that her mother—her "best friend"—gave all her love and energy to her children.[10] That love was revealed in the many scrapbooks Mary Hanford kept. Into each of these scrapbooks, she carefully placed photographs, school projects, report cards, and other papers detailing her children's lives. Almost two dozen of the scrapbooks chronicle the life of her daughter Elizabeth.

The family's Christian faith was also very strong. Each Sunday Elizabeth visited her grandmother, Cora Alexander Cathey. There, "Mom Cathey" would tell stories she knew from the Bible, which she read every day. She set an even more dramatic example of faith and charity when one of her sons was killed in an automobile accident. Instead of keeping the life insurance money, Mom Cathey sent it to Pakistan, where it was used to expand a hospital run by Christian missionaries. In an interview Dole gave many years later, she recalled "My grandmother taught me that what we do on our own matters little—what counts is what God chooses to do through us. She stressed the importance of ministering to others and Jesus' instruction to his followers to 'Feed my sheep.'" [11]

Into this loving, religious, hard-working family, Elizabeth Hanford was born in 1936, the day before her father's birthday. It was also three days before the local hospital opened its new building. The nursery in the old building had already been shut down, leaving no place to put the newborn baby. Her father had to dash home in his car to get a bassinet and bring it back to the hospital.

The new baby dazzled those who saw her. The baby book her mother kept includes glowing notes about Elizabeth. The doctor who delivered the baby called her "very pretty." The nurse wrote, "This is to certify that Elizabeth Alexander Hanford is the best little baby I have ever cared for. Her habits from the beginning of life being near perfect." [12] Three days after her birth, Elizabeth was moved, along with her mother and the nurse, to the new hospital. On the drive, they were serenaded by the tunes of a music box.

Even as a young girl, Elizabeth—then known as "Liddy"—strived for perfection. The second child of John and Mary Hanford, Elizabeth was raised to be disciplined and productive, but she put more pressure on herself than anyone else. One of her teachers told a reporter that as a child, the future senator "wanted to please so bad."

The three older Hanfords had disagreed on what to name the new baby. Her father and brother, both Johns, wanted to name her after Mary, her mother. But Mrs. Hanford wanted to pay tribute to her own grandmother by naming the child Elizabeth Alexander. The couple finally hit on a compromise, calling her Mary Elizabeth Alexander Hanford. But through most of her childhood, Elizabeth went by another name—Liddy. She gave herself that name when she was 18 months old. Her mother was looking for her and called out "Elizabeth, where are you?" The toddler called back, "Here Lidie,"[13] and the name stuck. To this day, family and school friends from Salisbury still call her Liddy. Most people she met later in life call her Elizabeth.

Young Liddy was a forceful child from the start. At age one, her mother noted, "She is very willful and insists on having her own way."[14] Nonetheless, her parents believed in discipline. When she was two, they spanked her on two or three occasions because she had not shared toys or behaved nicely with other children. Those punishments put a stop to the misbehavior. She had one other brush with punishment. Once she had to confess to pasting pictures on the walls of her room. Her father took her to each picture and asked her point-blank if she had put it there. "After each admission," she recalled in her autobiography, "I was given a few pats with a broomstraw switch. They hurt much less than the thought of having disappointed this man whom I loved so much."[15]

Even as a young child, Elizabeth Dole hated making mistakes. Once in second grade, she forgot to bring a book to school, and her teacher sent her back home to get it. She cried all the way home, shamed by her oversight.

In this and many other traits, Dole's character reflects the influence of her parents. Her father was very well organized. He would awaken each morning before the rest of the family and sit down to make to-do lists of all the things he wanted to accomplish that day. Similarly, his daughter has a reputation for always being completely prepared for public events. Some people criticize her as a perfectionist. Her brother John finds such faultfinding baffling. "What's wrong with trying to be perfect?" he once asked a reporter.[16]

From her mother, Dole learned to be disciplined enough to use her time productively. When Elizabeth finished her homework, her mother suggested she do extra practice on the piano.

Her mother also taught her to lead an active life. Mary Cathey Hanford was involved in her church, in the Parent Teacher Association, and in other community groups. She also helped out at the family florist shop, answering phones, designing arrangements, and doing similar tasks. Her days were full, and she met her commitments with dedication. "Mother has never tackled anything," Dole writes, "without giving it her all." [17] Her daughter was just as active. As a child, along with piano and religious classes, she belonged to a group called the Children of the American Revolution. In high school, she worked in student government, the dramatics club, and the school newspaper. In high school, she joined other students in selling magazine subscriptions to raise money for activities. Elizabeth, of course, sold more than anyone else. The secret to her success was to sell the subscriptions to grandmothers who were eager to help their grandchildren. Even when she had fun, she was busy doing it. A high school boyfriend who had dated her told a reporter, "She would plumb wear me out. She wanted to do more things. I really could not keep up with her. If we went to dinner, she wanted to go to a movie, then go bowling, then go play tennis." [18]

The Hanford children, despite a thirteen-year age difference, were very close. When Elizabeth was young, her brother John would hoist her up on his shoulders and carry her around while she held onto his hair. Once Liddy was on his shoulders, their mother recalled, she would "not go to anyone" else.[19] John's friends took a liking to his little sister. In fact, his high school graduating class affectionately voted her its "class mascot." When her schedule allows, she still takes part in their class reunions.

From her Grandmother Cathey, she gained a love for birds. Years later, when she was president of the Red Cross, she kept a bird feeder outside her office window. In fact, she loved animals of all kinds. According to her brother, she often brought home stray animals. Several became family pets.

Books were also a great part of Elizabeth Hanford's childhood. She enjoyed reading novels like *Anne of Green Gables* and *Heidi*. She also read inspirational books like *The Book of Success* and *Ideals of Great Men*. One summer she read forty books. In her autobiography, Dole admitted that one reason she read was because she liked getting good grades. A teacher told a reporter that she "wanted to please so bad." [20]

Her brother recalls that "she always emulated the adults." [21] This helped give her a maturity that many children lack, and from this maturity came a strong sense of responsibility. A local woman ran a program for youngsters as part of the group Children of the American Revolution. But the program met on Saturdays, the only day the children had free to themselves. Over time, fewer and fewer children came to the sessions. But Elizabeth kept going. "No one else wants to go," she told her family. "I've got to go help." [22]

Her teachers treasured her. Piano teacher Lillian Watkins once sent a note to the Hanford house praising her pupil. She wrote, "I wish it were possible to put into words the joy Liddy gives me as a pupil. She is always responsive to any suggestion and is such an intelligent, eager worker. She is an excellent 'planner' as she seems to know how to use her working time, as well as her spare time, well. All in all, she is just about unique, and any teacher would rejoice in having the opportunity of working with her." [23] High school teacher Bob Greenland told a reporter that she was "a wonderful student." [24]

Hard work and a quick mind brought Elizabeth many successes. When she was in sixth grade, a national radio show had a best teacher contest. Her mother suggested that she write a tribute to a teacher who had died and enter it in the contest. Her entry won a prize. The next year, she wrote an essay about an episode in the Civil War and won another contest. In eighth grade, she won her school's citizenship award, topping the achievement by winning another essay contest soon after. She was talented musically, too. She played the piano so well that the church invited her to play each Sunday for the Bible-study classes of younger children.

In athletics and other physical activities, Elizabeth Hanford was less talented. She went to dance classes for a while but was not very good at it. "Mary," her father asked her mother during one dance recital, "why in the world did you encourage her to take ballet?"[25] In her memoir, she described her lack of ability at sports humorously. "Wearing glasses was no help on the baseball diamond," she writes, "and my disdain for the American Game (perhaps brought on by embarrassment over line drives dropped) prompted me to stay home from school once or twice."[26]

She was also not very talented at such traditional women's activities as cooking and sewing. "The kitchen was not my natural habitat," she recalls.[27] High school home economics classes were a source of high stress. She grew worried after failing on seven attempts at sewing a zipper into a skirt. Her anxiety resulted from a rumor that girls could not graduate from her high school if they could not sew. Fortunately, a friend's mother helped her master the technique, and she was able to complete the assignment.

Such setbacks were rare, and Elizabeth was often able to turn adversity into something positive—sometimes with her family's help. One day Elizabeth complained that she was always chosen last when children formed softball teams. Her mother quickly pointed out that she was always picked first for spelling teams. When she was three, a doctor told the family that she needed glasses. The news upset her mother, who worried that glasses would spoil her daughter's appearance, especially when she became old enough to wear formal gowns (contact lenses were not yet widely available). Her father helped reconcile Elizabeth to the idea of glasses by pointing out that it was something the two of them shared exclusively, something that set them apart from her mother and brother. Later, when she was older, she borrowed model paint from her brother and painted the frames of the glasses different colors so they would match the dress she was wearing at any given time. When she wore formal gowns, she left her glasses at home.

Among Elizabeth's talents was leadership ability. Other children often picked her to be a group leader. In third grade, she formed a bird club and became president. In the early 1940s, while the nation fought World War II, she organized some elementary school classmates into a small group that gathered materials such as tinfoil and used postage stamps. They were, the local newspaper said, the youngest "defense group" in the town. In junior high, she organized a book club. This time, she did not bother to wait for a vote. She simply named herself president.

Leadership continued in later grades. She was president of the youth group at church and president of her high school class. As childhood friend Tyson Underwood told a newspaper reporter, "It was just understood that she had leadership qualities. She was a good example of that Southern trait that if you had ability and talent, you accepted the responsibilities thrust on you. If you were capable and other people felt you were needed in a job, you were obliged to do the best you could in it." [28]

A friend recalled that classmates teased Elizabeth that she would become the first woman president. The idea was apparently not completely foreign to her. One night, while she was still in high school, she and a boy she was dating sat on the banks of a river, talking. That night, she told the boy, "You know what? I want to be the first woman president of the United States." [29] Clearly, the intelligent, energetic young woman also had ambition.

One way that Elizabeth showed leadership was by avoiding any haughtiness towards others. The Hanfords were one of the better families in town, a family that was well off and well established in the area. But Elizabeth never treated other children as though she were better. Harold Isenberg, then principal of her elementary school, recalled that when she chose friends "it made no difference where they lived or what their parents did."[30] Indeed, she often tried to help children who were less fortunate, showing the generosity that she had learned from her grandmother. At lunchtime, she frequently offered to trade her well-prepared meals for the food of students who had smaller, less elaborate lunches. Her parents had a credit arrangement at the local drugstore. She could buy a few dollars worth of goods each month without paying. Then her parents would settle the bill with the storeowner. One month, her mother was amazed that her daughter had spent $12 on comic books. Elizabeth explained that she had charged many of the books for her friends.

Her generous spirit extended to her family, too. During World War II, her brother John served in the navy. Every day, her mother haunted the mailbox, hoping to get a new letter from her faraway son. Too young to understand a mother's worry about the perils of war, Dole could only see that getting mail was important to her mother. When she went to camp that summer, she made sure to send her mother a letter every day.

Elizabeth Hanford grew up in a town that was comfortable and safe. In her autobiography, she described Salisbury as a quiet, loving, tranquil place:

> The pace of life was a little slower [there], the greeting extended to a stranger a little warmer, than in Northern cities. Salisbury is still the kind of place where people on the street tip their hat in welcome. . . . You don't need a holiday as an excuse to fly the flag. And families mean a lot, in part for their own camaraderie, but also for the foundation they lay for other relationships."[31]

But Salisbury was, in some respects, a narrow world. Her Cathey grandparents lived just two houses down the street. Her elementary school was just four blocks from home. The high school was even closer.

The Hanfords, who enjoyed seeing other places, expanded this narrow world through travel. After World War II, the family took several summer vacations. They traveled to Niagara Falls and Quebec. They went to the Rockies and the Northwest. From these travels, Elizabeth developed a desire to visit new places and see new sights. Yet she also retained an abiding love for Salisbury. "It's a town of wonderful people who support you in your joys and sorrows," she once said.[32]

There were major changes taking place in the world, but in some respects they got little notice in Salisbury. Elizabeth spent her first years of life in the waning years of the Depression, but she was too young to be aware of the hardships caused by that economic disaster, particularly as her own family remained prosperous. The 1940s were a time of war, but the conflict ended happily for the Hanfords when young John came home from the navy unharmed. The cold war followed, but it did not touch Salisbury deeply. Liddy's father built a fallout shelter for the family to hide in if a nuclear war broke out, but there was no major anxiety. As she wrote in her memoir, "Townspeople generally went about their business as usual. The daily patterns of small-town life gave most people the reassurance they were denied in the headlines."[33] There was also little notice in this small town—at least among the Hanfords—of the growing Civil Rights movement.

Society was different in Elizabeth Hanford's early years from society in the early twenty-first century. Girls wore dresses, not slacks or shorts, and almost no one wore jeans to school. Boys and girls were treated differently and raised differently. Girls were expected to learn to be charming and good homemakers. They were not expected to have careers.

But Liddy Hanford was ambitious, and this gender-specific treatment sometimes got in her way. Her high school had never had a female president of the entire student body. In her senior year, she ran for that office. But the majority of students were not willing to break tradition. They elected the male candidate instead of her. In her autobiography, Dole looked back on the experience as "a lesson in how to lose, something no one likes but from which most of us can benefit."[34]

By 1954, Elizabeth Hanford was ready to move on from Salisbury. She graduated from Boyden High School that year with excellent grades. Her achievements were recognized by school officials, and she was chosen as one of the

THE CIVIL RIGHTS MOVEMENT

For many decades, African Americans in the United States had suffered from prejudice and discrimination. Many whites believed that blacks did not have the same abilities as whites. Laws created by white-run governments denied full equality to blacks. African Americans had to ride in separate streetcars, buses, and trains from whites. They had to go to separate restaurants and hotels. They were forced to sit in separate areas in theaters and to use "colored only" public bathrooms and drinking fountains. To make sure that blacks could do nothing about these laws, whites passed other laws that made it impossible—or nearly so—for African Americans to vote.

During World War II, tens of thousands of young African-American men joined the armed services. Many, returning home after risking their lives in war, were disgusted by the unfair treatment they had to suffer. Emboldened by their wartime service to their country, they helped launch a concerted effort to bring about change. The late 1940s and early 1950s saw the beginning of the Civil Rights movement. In this effort, African Americans used protests, marches, demonstrations, and legal action to try to gain equal rights.

few students to give a speech at graduation. Her high school classmates recognized her abilities, too. They voted her the girl most likely to succeed.

The next step in that success would be college. Elizabeth would go to Duke University, a top-flight school in Durham, North Carolina. It was the same school her brother had attended, and it was the only college to which she had applied.

3

A Remarkable Education

1954–1965

Women share with men the need for personal success, even the taste of power, and no longer are we willing to satisfy those needs through the achievements of surrogates—whether husbands, children, or merely role models.

—Elizabeth Dole

In the fall of 1954, Elizabeth Hanford entered the freshman class of Duke University. At the time, the university housed two undergraduate colleges. Men attended Trinity College and lived on the West Campus. Hanford entered Woman's College and lived with other female students on the East Campus.

College life was much more formal then than it is today. Women students at Duke were called "Duchesses." They were given a handbook that outlined the behavior expected of them. It included such statements as "A Duchess should have tact and good judgment to know when the occasion requires her to be serious and when to be gay, when to dress up and when to be casual. Everything she does is in good taste and up to the highest standards."[35] Knowing "when to be casual" meant knowing that women did not wear jeans. They could wear shorts, but only on the East Campus. They could wear slacks, but never to classes.

The college also looked out for the women students' morals. They were required to take a religion class in their first year. The women's dormitories were closed at 10:30 P.M. Monday through Thursday, though they were open an extra hour on Friday, Saturday, and Sunday. Women had to be inside the dorms before then or face punishment.

At the same time, women students were expected to study. Alice Baldwin, dean of Woman's College from its formation in 1926 until 1947, had made sure that Duchesses took their education seriously. Admission was highly selective, meaning that only the best students were accepted. Florence Brinkley, who served as dean when Hanford was at Duke, carried on Baldwin's tradition. The former student remembers her fondly as "a tall, stately woman . . . [with] an almost maternal warmth." Dean Brinkley, Dole continues, "taught her students to think for themselves, and to think hard."[36]

Liddy Hanford loved the university from the start. Her first letter home told her parents that she was "crazy" about Duke. She also let them know that she was thinking about majoring in political science. That choice worried her mother, who thought that home economics would be more suitable— despite her daughter's problems with that subject in high school. Her anxious mother called a college professor to ask his advice. He calmed her down, saying that political science would be a good idea since the country needed more women in government. "Anyway," he reassured her, female college students "all get married eventually."[37]

Though such a statement might seem outrageous today, in the 1950s it was not far from the mark. A fellow student remembered that "there was much emphasis on dating and getting an engagement ring."[38] A childhood friend of Liddy's recalled, "You didn't think a woman would do anything but get married—that was the best thing you could do."[39] Social life was important on campus, and Hanford enjoyed it. She dated and went to football games. She made her social debut at a formal ball held in Raleigh—an event she "vaguely remember[s] as a haze of satin and chiffon."[40] In her sophomore year, she joined Delta Delta Delta, a sorority that combined social events with community service. Her dedication to service work continued in other ways. Junior year, she was named to the Freshman Advisory Council, which made her an advisor to first-year students.

Elizabeth also enjoyed several extracurricular activities. She sang in the Women's Glee Club and Chapel Choir her first two years at the university. She also worked on the business staff of the school yearbook. During her junior year, she worked on the technical crew of the Duke Players, a dramatics group.

Liddy also became heavily involved in student government. She ran for a position on the council of the Women's Student Government Association her first year at Duke. Later in life, she ruefully called her campaign speech a bit "overwrought"—in it, she compared her fellow students to Rip Van Winkle.[41] The campaign led to a stinging defeat, but she ran again, and in her junior and senior years she was elected to the council. As a senior, she became council president. A hometown friend and fellow Duke student once explained to a reporter why Liddy Hanford won that election. "She made friends along the way," her friend said. "When it came time for [the vote], she had a lot of support."[42]

Years later, Dole fondly remembered one accomplishment from her tenure as council president. Under her leadership, the council convinced school administrators to extend the Saturday curfew for women to one o'clock Sunday morning. Less successful was an effort to bring a student honor code to the university. Women supported the idea overwhelmingly— 96 percent voted for it. But the Duke men did not approve it, and the code was not adopted.

Liddy Hanford earned many honors during her college experience. In her second year, she was named as a member of Sandals, an honorary group. The women chosen for this group were those who showed leadership and a record of service. In her junior year, she was selected as student marshal for the school's graduation ceremonies. As a senior, she was one of only a few women selected to join an honorary women's group called White Duchy. She also earned a place in Phi Beta Kappa, an honorary academic society that accepts students on the basis of good grades. That same year, the student newspaper named her "Leader of the Year." Duke's women students voted her the May Queen, an honor based on a combination of beauty, service, and personal achievement. When she graduated, in 1958, she was the only one of 37 seniors in the political science department who received a diploma stating that she had graduated "with distinction."

After an active and involved four years of college, Liddy Hanford was not sure what to do with her life. One thing she was sure of—she did not wish to get married. She had dated a young man from nearby Davidson College, and he had given her his fraternity pin. This signaled a serious relationship, and mutual friend Peggy Looney once told a reporter that the two were very much in love. But the young man, Richard Jones, wanted to return to his hometown of Franklin, North Carolina, and practice law. "I don't think," Looney told a reporter, "that was the way Liddy wanted to spend her life." Dole revealed little about this experience in her autobiography. She simply said, "Though I cared for him very much, I simply was not ready for marriage."[43] In an interview with a *Washington Post* reporter, though, she elaborated:

> You know practically every young woman that I had graduated high school with and college just went right into marriage and settling down. And I suddenly thought, 'Whoa, wait a minute, I'm not ready to get a ring here.' This fraternity pin's very nice but when you're talking about a ring that's pretty serious. I just felt this pull to live in another part of the country and to broaden my horizons and to go to graduate school. There were so many things I wanted to do."[44]

At any rate, she broke up with the young man.

The desire to experience new things also prompted Liddy to turn down another offer. Her brother John—now working in the family florist business—offered her a job with the company. Although the job would have allowed her to travel to foreign countries, which appealed to her, she declined. She hoped to join the staff of the *Charlotte Observer*, a local newspaper. Confident from years of success that she would get a job simply by showing up, she was disappointed when she was not hired. She learned a lesson from this, and she later wrote: "If you couldn't, or wouldn't, make the case for why you should get the job, you could hardly expect a prospective boss to make it for you."[45]

Casting about for something to do, Liddy Hanford made a radical decision for a young woman from North Carolina. She moved to New England, settling in Cambridge, Massachusetts. There she got a job as secretary to the head librarian of Harvard University's Law School. She was fortunate to get the job. She could not take shorthand, a common skill among secretaries at the time, and she was not very good at typing. At night, she later said, she had to retype "all the things I hadn't gotten quite right during the day."[46]

Sitting under the blossoming trees as Duke University's May Queen in this 1958 photo, the attractive Elizabeth Hanford seems to embody the ideal of womanhood in the 1950s. Yet Elizabeth's appearance belies her many scholarly accomplishments, including acceptance into the prestigious Phi Beta Kappa academic society. After Duke, Elizabeth would earn both a master's degree and a law degree from Harvard, rejecting the domestic role women from her generation were expected to take.

Still, the job went well and had several advantages. No longer needing to do homework, Hanford was free to enjoy herself on evenings and weekends. When family or friends visited, she showed them the historic and cultural sights of Boston and its surrounding area. She had learned to enjoy skiing on a summer trip to Colorado while in college, so she took some trips into northern New England to sample the ski slopes of Vermont. Another advantage of the Law School job was that it kept her on a student's schedule. This meant that she had summers off. In the summer of 1959, she traveled to England, where she took courses at Oxford University. She also had some fun, staying out so late one night that the gates to the dormitory were closed when she returned. She had to scale the wall to get back in.

When Liddy's studies ended, she still some free had time before she had to return to her job. She decided to embark on yet another adventure. She wanted to travel to Moscow, capital of the Soviet Union. She knew that convincing her parents to let her go would be difficult. She prepared by filling a piece of paper with the arguments she would use to overcome their opposition. The transatlantic phone call was difficult, but in the end the daughter won. She made the trip and suffered none of the problems her parents had worried about. She even managed to spend one night in the apartment of a Russian she had met, giving her a chance to observe ordinary people. While in the apartment, she noticed that the friend's mother kept her radio playing at high volume all evening long. The woman was not listening to music; she was using the noise to drown out the sound of their conversation in case someone else was listening in. The stark contrast to the freedom she knew back in the United States struck Liddy Hanford deeply.

Back in Cambridge in the fall of 1959, Liddy Hanford decided to enroll in Harvard's School of Education. She entered a program that combined the study of government with the study of teaching. "The first was my emerging passion," she wrote later, "the second a vocational insurance policy."[47] Her student teaching assignment was an eleventh grade history class in a nearby suburb. Liddy brought energy and imagination to her the work. Hoping to make history come alive for her students, she brought in local people who had lived through some of the events the class was studying. After a year, she received her joint masters degree.

Once again, graduation posed an important question: what next? Her professors urged her to continue teaching, but Hanford was not committed to the profession. She admired teachers greatly, but did not see herself as one. She felt that government work would be more interesting. So in the summer of 1960, degree in hand, she traveled to Washington, D.C. She showed up at the office of B. Everett Jordan, one of North Carolina's two senators, and announced that she wanted to work for him. Years later, Jordan's chief of staff told a reporter that they decided to hire her because she had gone to

THE COLD WAR

Elizabeth Hanford's parents' worries about her traveling to Moscow might seem strange now, but in the late 1950s and early 1960s, the United States and the Soviet Union were locked in a bitter struggle. The two superpowers vied against each other to win influence with other countries in the world. On more than one occasion, each side became involved in fighting against countries allied with the other side. But because they never sent their armies directly against each other, the conflict was known as the "cold war."

All during the cold war, many people worried that the rivalry between the United States and the Soviet Union could develop into a nuclear war. Both sides possessed large arsenals of nuclear weapons. Each could easily destroy the major cities of the other. In 1959, many Americans deeply mistrusted the Soviets and their leader, Nikita Khrushchev.

Liddy Hanford was hoping to visit Moscow at the same time Khrushchev was visiting the United States. The timing increased her parents' anxieties. If anything should happen to the Soviet leader while he was in the United States, they worried, Americans in Moscow would be in danger. Fortunately, nothing happened to either visitor.

Duke, as Jordan had done, and they had no one else from Duke on the staff.

What began as a summer job turned into an exciting political adventure when John F. Kennedy won the Democratic Party's nomination for the presidency. The chief of staff was good friends with Lyndon Baines Johnson, the powerful senator from Texas who became the Democratic Party's nominee for vice president. Through this connection, Liddy Hanford came to work on a weeklong campaign swing, traveling by train with the vice presidential candidate and other Kennedy-Johnson supporters. It was her first exposure to an election campaign, and she found it an exciting "blur of cheering crowds [and] rear-platform speechmaking."[48]

In the fall, Liddy was back in Cambridge, working at the law school again. This time, though, she had to think about a piece of advice she had received. During her Washington summer, she had sought the advice of Margaret Chase Smith. The famous Maine politician was, at the time, the only woman in the U.S. Senate. Liddy Hanford brashly knocked on her door one day, armed with a number of questions. Smith graciously agreed to answer them—an act that Elizabeth Dole remembers fondly today and tries to repeat when young women call on her for the same reason. One thing Smith told her was to go to law school. If she really wanted a career in government, Smith said, a law degree would be a great help.

Liddy Hanford spent the fall of 1960 through the summer of 1962 the same way. She worked at the law school during the school year. In the summers, she worked at the United Nations in New York City. That job came about when she showed the same audacity that led her to Senator Jordan's office looking for work and to Senator Smith's office seeking advice. She ignored warnings that the UN had no openings for summer workers and went to the job office. There she pointedly said that she wanted only summer work, adding that she was very committed to working at the UN. The brash approach worked, and she got a job giving tours to visiting groups.

During one of those summers, Liddy Hanford broke up with another boyfriend, a fellow North Carolinian who was studying at Harvard's Medical School. On a visit he made to New York City, it became clear that the two had serious differences. They decided to part.

Once again, Elizabeth Hanford was not sure what to do with her life. It was 1962 and she was nearly 26 years old. In May of that year, she had a reminder of her selection as May Queen back at Duke. The local command of the U.S. Navy staged something called the "Space Age Frolics," and she was chosen queen of the event. As a result of this honor, she was photographed with the pitchers from the Boston Red Sox baseball team. In her autobiography, Elizabeth Dole viewed this as something of a turning point. "Baseball players have short careers," she says, "but so do women who wear cardboard crowns. I was getting a little old for this sort of thing." [49]

Two colleagues at the library suggested that Liddy should apply to Harvard Law School. This was, of course, the same advice she had been given by Senator Smith two years earlier. By this time, she had met plenty of law students, and she had confidence that she was as intelligent as most of them. Her brother argued that law school would be like spending three years in a monastery, but she decided to give it a try.

Telling her parents about the decision proved difficult. They came up to New England to visit, and they and Elizabeth took a brief holiday to New Hampshire. There, she delivered the news. Her mother did not like the idea at first. "Don't you want to be a wife, and a mother, and a hostess for your husband?" she asked. [50] Her daughter replied that she did want to be all those things—but not yet. Her parents agreed to the plan, but not without misgivings. That night, Liddy heard her distraught mother throwing up in the bathroom.

Liddy Hanford was accepted by Harvard Law School, and

in the fall of 1962, she returned to the campus, not as an employee but as a student. She faced a stiff challenge. Professors were demanding, and the courses were rigorous. Homework required many hours of reading. Students were often highly competitive, and some did nothing to help fellow students who struggled. Indeed, some tried to make life more difficult for other students so their own performance would look better.

Women students faced even more difficulties. Classmate Elizabeth Holtzman—later a member of Congress from New York—recalled that the school had "an institutional hostility to women." [51] Harvard Law had begun admitting women students only a decade or so before Hanford and Holtzman enrolled, and Harvard professors did not extend a warm welcome to female students. Most refused to call on any women in their classes, except one day a year. In Dole's memoir, she recalled this "public humiliation" in her class on property law:

> The only exception was an annual display known as Professor Leach's Ladies' Day, when the women in property were summoned to the front of the room to read a poem of their own composition. Once this ritual was over, Professor Leach, seated with the male students, would pelt us with questions. [52]

Dole resented how dehumanizing the school was for women. Some years later, she shared a speaker's podium with the man who had been dean during her student years. The bitterness of her experience boiled over as she peppered the former dean with questions about the treatment of women students.

Male classmates were not very supportive of women students either. On the first day of classes, she was berated by a male student. "What are you doing here?" he asked. "Don't you realize there are *men* who would give their right arm to be in this law school, men who would *use* their legal education?" [53]

breezily. In the evenings, she says, she cooked Japanese food for guests. "During the day," she added, "I left the kitchen and looked for a job through government employment offices."[57] The comment makes light of what was probably a difficult time. Elizabeth Hanford was still searching for her path in life. She knew she did not want to become a corporate lawyer, handling business law cases for wealthy clients. This was a typical career for Harvard Law graduates, but not for her. She was committed to government work—doing something for the public good. But it took many months for her to find a suitable job. In the meantime, she had to keep her spirits up. She also had to study for the Washington, D.C., bar exam. This is the test law school graduates must pass in order to gain a license to practice law. Crucial to a law career, the test is also grueling, lasting many hours.

In early 1966, Elizabeth Hanford had two successes. She passed the D.C. bar exam and found a job, though only a temporary one. The Department of Health, Education and Welfare (HEW) hired her in a low-level professional position.

Elizabeth's chief assignment was to plan a conference on educating the deaf, which would be held in 1967. It would be the first such conference the government had ever held, so she had to develop it from scratch. She spent the next months researching the issue and identifying the topics to cover. Then she lined up speakers to fill the meeting time. Finally, in the spring of 1967, the conference was held in Colorado Springs, Colorado. Soon after, the temporary position ended, and she was back job hunting once again.

While looking for more permanent work, Elizabeth decided to become a public defender. Public defenders are lawyers who defend people accused of committing a crime. Because they do not charge for the work, they represent people who cannot otherwise afford legal help. Elizabeth Hanford thought that doing such work would be good experience as well as benefiting the people who needed it.

Elizabeth did not feel ready to jump right in to this sort of work. She had no experience in the courtroom and had been out of law school for two years. She felt she needed some training before taking any cases. While looking for a job during the day, she went to the city's night court to watch proceedings. On her third night there, she was startled to find Judge Edward Beard pointing at her and asking, "Who are you?" After she identified herself, the judge asked what she was doing there.

"I'm observing the proceedings, Your Honor, so that I can take cases," she responded.

The judge then asked if she had passed the bar. Hearing that she had, he told her he had a case for her. Surprised and anxious, Elizabeth told the judge she was not ready to handle a case. Judge Beard dismissed her concerns, saying, "If you are a member of the D.C. bar, Miss Hanford, you are ready to take a case." [58]

In this way, Elizabeth Hanford began working as a public defender. Her first case was comical. She had to defend someone accused of annoying a lion at the National Zoo in Washington. The defendant, a Greek man who spoke little English, did not understand the charges against him. Wanting time to prepare the case, Elizabeth hoped to postpone the trial to another day. The defendant would not agree to that, however; he wanted to return to New York City the next day. Soon after hearing that, Elizabeth Hanford and her client were summoned to the courtroom—the judge was ready for the trial to get underway. Realizing that she had no choice, she nervously entered the courtroom. There she found herself facing not only a tough and demanding judge, but also a formidable legal opponent. The prosecuting attorney had been one of the best students in her Harvard Law class.

Elizabeth tried a novel argument. Without testimony from the lion, she said, the court could not know if the animal had actually been annoyed. The prosecutor pointed out that the man had been found once before in an animal's cage. He charged that the man was a danger to the zoo. The judge asked the defendant to swear that he would never visit the National Zoo again. At Elizabeth's urging, the defendant promised, winning his release. "Not bad for the first time out of the box," the judge told Elizabeth.[59]

For the next year, Elizabeth worked as a public defender. The experience opened her eyes to many people she had never seen in Salisbury, at Duke, or at Harvard. Some were addicted to drugs. Some were tough people accused of armed robbery. Dole recalls the year as "sometimes hilarious, more often heartrending, but never dull."[60]

While handling these cases, Elizabeth still hoped to get a job in the government. In 1968, she learned of an exciting opportunity. Lyndon Johnson's administration was opening a new office, the White House Office of Consumer Affairs. Workers were needed to fill the staff, and Elizabeth jumped at the chance. She saw this as an opportunity to help people in a different way and to become part of the growing consumer movement. She might also have shrewdly figured that a new field like consumer rights offered a good opportunity for someone to rise faster in the government than a more established field.

To get the job, Elizabeth Hanford had to have an interview with John Macy, head of the Civil Service Commission. He had been one of the three-member panel that had decided on the White House fellowships three years earlier. Macy was apparently impressed by Hanford, and he was eager to bring more women and minority-group members into government. There was one serious obstacle. The Office of Consumer Affairs did not have a budget for the job Elizabeth wanted. She had to find another government agency that could hire her on its budget and then loan her to the White House. Fortunately, she had a useful contact. While working at HEW, she had met James Goddard, who was the head of the Food and Drug Administration (FDA), a major federal agency. More importantly, Goddard was interested in consumer issues.

Elizabeth convinced Goddard to hire her and, as a result, began working in the White House.

After just a few months on the job, Elizabeth Hanford faced uncertainty once again. In November 1968, the United States elected a new president. Democrat Lyndon Johnson— who had backed consumer rights—was leaving office. The new

THE CONSUMER MOVEMENT

In the late 1800s and early 1900s, several journalists published stories describing abuses of power by giant corporations. Some companies schemed to keep prices high. Some used tough tactics to eliminate competitors. Many factories forced people to work under very harsh and dangerous conditions. These stories led the government to pass laws aimed at protecting consumers.

Interest in consumer issues dropped off after the early 1900s. The attitude could be summed up in the saying *caveat emptor*. This Latin phrase means "let the buyer beware." Few new consumer laws were passed.

In the 1960s, though, some people began a renewed push for laws protecting consumers. This movement got a boost in 1965. That year, lawyer Ralph Nader published *Unsafe at Any Speed*. His book showed that Chevrolet's Corvair, a sports car, was extremely unsafe, which led to many deadly accidents. Nader also revealed that the company knew the car was unsafe and did nothing about it. Soon after, Congress passed a law giving the government the power to make sure that cars were safe.

Consumer advocates also pushed other issues in the 1960s. They looked carefully at the safety of other products. They complained about misleading ads that tricked consumers. They pointed out unfair business practices in the credit industry, the businesses that loan money to consumers. As a result, Congress passed other laws that gave consumers protections in these areas.

covered certain construction problems for a period of time. In her speech, Hanford urged more builders to offer such warranties. She also warned them that they could not ignore the issue:

> The patience of the American consumer is rapidly running out. . . . There are many cases—and home building is certainly one of them—where consumers are demanding more protection from government, not less. . . . As homebuilders, you have a choice: either you can each independently decide to make self-regulation work or you can brace yourselves for full-scale, hard-hitting regulation from the government.[63]

Working as an FTC commissioner was an important step in Elizabeth Hanford's career. The year after she joined the commission, *Time* magazine included her in a list of 200 people identified as "faces for the future." During the 1970s, she also had an important change in her personal life. In 1972, Virginia Knauer had introduced her to Bob Dole, a senator from Kansas. Their first meeting was business related. Knauer wanted the Republican Party to take a stand in favor of consumer rights. She hoped Hanford could convince Dole—then chairman of the Republican Party—to back that position. But Knauer also thought that these two friends of hers would be suited to each other.

Bob Dole had been an officer in the army during World War II. In a battle in Italy, he suffered severe wounds that left him paralyzed. Over four years, and after three operations, he was able to regain the ability to move most of his body. His right arm and hand remained paralyzed. Dole eventually returned to his home in Kansas and studied law. Entering politics, he was elected to the U.S. House of Representatives four times. In 1968, he was first elected to the Senate. He was divorced and had a grown daughter from his first marriage.

Elizabeth Hanford married Bob Dole on December 6, 1975, in the National Cathedral of Washington, D.C. The pair met in 1972 when Hanford, who was working for the Federal Trade Commission, wanted to persuade Dole, a prominent senator, to support consumer rights. The marriage of these two influential government employees began a political partnership that would last throughout their lives; both Bob and Elizabeth would rely on each other during their respective bids at elected offices.

Dole and Hanford met a few times in the summer of 1972. They also spoke on the phone a few times—though those conversations were social, not business. On the third call, the senator finally asked Hanford for a date. Concerned that she might turn him down because he was 13 years older, he had been hesitant to ask her earlier. But Hanford thought the senator was interesting. She saw him as handsome and also a bit shy—something she found refreshing in Washington, D.C., where many men are pushy. She also liked his wit. Elizabeth also had a keen sense of humor, a fact that gave Knauer the idea she and Bob Dole would be good together.

Their first dinner together went well, and the two continued dating. By 1974, they had become more serious. Dole was campaigning for re-election that year and was forced to spend a great deal of time out of Washington. Each night he was on the road, though, he would call Hanford at the end of the day. That fall, she took a trip to Japan. When she returned home, she found a welcome-back present of flowers and champagne. At that point, she writes, "I knew that things were getting serious." Soon after, they decided to marry. In her memoir, Dole wrote that she could not remember the senator making a formal proposal. Instead, she said, "we just gradually began to think of the future as something we wanted to share. We were happier together than apart."[64]

Elizabeth Hanford and Bob Dole were married on December 6, 1975. The ceremony was held in a chapel in Washington's National Cathedral. As both their fathers were ill at the time, the wedding was a small and simple. Elizabeth Dole related in her autobiography that the groom spoke the words "I do" a bit early in the ceremony. Still, the wedding continued, and the couple exchanged their vows. The reception afterward was very large and festive. At each diner's place was a mocked-up copy of the Congressional Record, the official proceedings of Congress, with a story about the wedding.

The couple went on a honeymoon, which was cut short by the death of Bob Dole's father. It was a sad ending to what had been a happy time for the newlyweds.

Washington's Power Couple

1975–1987

Sometimes I think we're the only two lawyers in Washington who trust each other.

—Elizabeth Dole about her marriage
to Bob Dole in *Newsweek*, 1987

The Doles became one of Washington, D.C.'s "power couples," a term frequently used to describe married people who both have high-level government jobs. Both became important figures in the Republican Party. This brought some unusual changes to Elizabeth Hanford Dole's life. The Catheys had always voted Democratic. The Hanfords had also been staunch Democrats although Elizabeth's father had switched his allegiance to the Republican Party in the 1950s. As a result, Elizabeth Hanford had begun her political life as a Democrat. When she became part of the Republican White House under President Richard Nixon, she changed her political status to "independent," meaning a person who does not belong to any political party. One day, before the Doles married, the senator read a newspaper article that pointed this out. "You're a *what?*" he asked in shock.[65] Shortly before the wedding, she switched to the Republican Party.

By this time, in the 1970s, such a move was not considered radical. The Democratic Party of the South had traditionally been fairly conservative. Southern Democrats did not favor a strong national government and wanted low taxes. In the 1960s and 1970s, these ideas became central beliefs of the Republican Party. Many people in the Democratic Party, meanwhile, had begun to support large government programs and were willing, if necessary, to pay for them through higher taxes. As a result, many Southern Democrats did the same thing Elizabeth Dole had done and switched parties.

The Doles were thrust deeply into party politics just a few months after marrying. In the summer of 1976, Gerald Ford won the presidential nomination of the Republican Party. During the party's national convention that August, he picked Senator Bob Dole as his vice presidential running mate. Word apparently leaked to the press from someone in the Ford campaign before the Doles had been told. They heard a buzz of reporters gathered in the hallway outside their room and wondered what was going on. Soon after, to Bob Dole's surprise, a reporter called the room to ask for the senator's reaction to the news of his candidacy. Dole had not even heard the news yet. When Ford finally did call to offer him the opportunity to run for vice president, the Kansas senator quickly accepted.

The Doles were honored by the choice but also a bit apprehensive. They knew they faced a grueling round of travel, speech-making, and special events that would disrupt their lives. They had been looking forward to taking a relaxing vacation after the convention, but, as Elizabeth Dole remembers, "thoughts of a tropical beach were dropped for more immediate concerns."[66] They were soon confronted with another measure of the change in their lives. Secret Service agents came to their room to provide the protection given to all candidates for president and vice president and their families. The Doles became "Ramrod" and "Rainbow," code names the agents used to refer to them for the rest of the campaign. Meanwhile, Elizabeth tried to call her parents back in Salisbury to warn them to look out for the press. She could not reach them, and reporters got to their home first.

Elizabeth could not stay in her FTC position and campaign for the Ford–Dole ticket at the same time. Unlike elected officials, other government workers are barred from engaging in politics. She took a leave of absence from the FTC for the duration of the campaign.

The campaign itself was as tiring as they had expected. Bob Dole's description of a presidential campaign was "up before dawn each day, into a motorcade to catch an airplane waiting to whisk you to three media-market cities, more motorcades and flashing lights—anything to get a cameraman to snap your picture or a network anchorman to put you on the evening news for ten seconds." [67]

There were also difficult issues the couple had to wrestle with, including what role Elizabeth would play. She recalled the dilemma in her memoir:

> Bob wanted me to campaign with him. Hoping to give whatever moral support I could. . . . I didn't want to leave the side of the man to whom I'd been married less than a year. . . . At the same time, I was under pressure from women at the Republican National Committee. . . . The best way to help Bob, they argued, was to carve out a separate campaign schedule and cover as much territory as possible. [68]

They chose a middle way. The Doles traveled to the same cities, but appeared at separate campaign events in each one. Then, at night, they reunited.

It was Elizabeth's first real taste of campaigning. She found it demanding and rewarding, humorous and taxing. She had to overcome her tendency to plan everything and always be prepared because there were constant surprises. The campaign also fascinated her, presenting what she calls "a civics lesson you can't possible get in the classroom or in Washington."[69] In the end, though, the Ford–Dole ticket lost. It was a close election, but Democrat Jimmy Carter became president and Walter Mondale became vice president. A few days later, candidate Bob Dole thanked his wife for her work. "I couldn't have gotten through this without you," he told her.[70]

After the election, Bob Dole returned to the Senate, and Elizabeth Dole went back to the FTC. They continued working in these jobs for the next few years. Sometimes they disagreed on issues. On one occasion, they appeared together in an interview debating whether a new consumer protection agency should be set up. Elizabeth argued for it; Bob argued against it. Many who had seen the show sent them letters afterward. Some criticized the female Dole for being too outspoken. Others, though, agreed with her.

In 1979, Senator Dole decided he would try to win the Republican Party's nomination for president. Once again, Elizabeth faced a career choice. She decided—under no pressure from her husband—to leave the FTC. Years later, she explained her thinking:

> A career is more than a paycheck: it's a series of learning opportunities. A national political campaign, with all its potential for growth as I discussed issues across the country with the press and the public, would be an unparalleled learning opportunity. I didn't rush to judgment. But I had no trouble making up my mind either.[71]

This time, instead of taking a leave of absence, she resigned from the FTC.

The Dole campaign did not muster much support. Former California Governor Ronald Reagan was winning far more votes than Senator Dole or the other Republican candidates. Early in 1980, Senator Dole dropped out of the race, deciding to run for re-election to the Senate. After Reagan won the Republican nomination, Elizabeth joined the former governor's campaign. She spent much of the next few months traveling, making speeches on his behalf. The 1980 elections resulted in a major Republican victory. Ronald Reagan won the presidency by a huge margin. At the same time, Republicans won control of the Senate for the first time in 30 years. When the Senate began a new session in 1981, Senator Dole had an important position. He became chairman of the Finance Committee, which oversees taxes. This committee also handles issues related to the Social Security program, which makes payments to retired people, and the Medicare and Medicaid programs, which pay for health care for some Americans.

Meanwhile, Elizabeth Dole was becoming part of the new administration. She accepted a job as head of the White House Office of Public Liaison. Staffers in this office contacted local and national groups, asking group members to send letters or make phone calls urging members of Congress to support the president's policies. Dole compares the office's work to a company's marketing and sales force. "Our job," she later said, "was to make sure the [White House's] ivory-tower types stayed in contact with the world beyond the gates, that organized groups had their views heard and considered, and that once official policy was determined it was supported."[72]

The office's first task was to win support across the country for Reagan's economic policies. The new president wanted to cut government spending while sharply cutting taxes. Elizabeth Dole organized her workers to convince many groups to give their support to these ideas. In the middle of July, the tax-cut plan came up to a vote in Congress. Dole's work paid off. In the last few days before the vote, more than a million phone calls

Dole became the first woman appointed to President Ronald Reagan's White House staff when she accepted a position heading the Office of Public Liaison. Through her post, Dole was able to continue in her mission as a public servant; the office listened to the needs of the American people, communicated them to the White House administration, and then promoted the policy developed in response. As the head of such an important organization, Dole quickly gained recognition as a powerful Republican woman.

came in to members of Congress backing the president's plan. With such strong support, Congress passed the tax cuts.

She also worked in the opposite direction—carrying messages from the people to the White House—to get another bill passed. The federal government buys many things from private companies. These include cars for government workers, paper and computers for offices, and food for soldiers. Until the 1980s, the government could delay payment for these goods for months at a time. This hurt the companies that sold the goods. Dole arranged a meeting between President Reagan and a group of business leaders unhappy about slow government payments. The business group quickly convinced the president to back a bill that would force the government to pay more promptly. Dole also worked to increase job opportunities for women.

In 1984, Ronald Reagan again won the presidency by a large vote. Elizabeth Dole—now a prominent Republican woman—campaigned hard for his re-election. She traveled more than 40,000 miles to more than half of the country's states, giving speeches and appearing at political events. In that election, Howard Baker left the Senate, opening up his position as majority leader. Republicans in the Senate chose Bob Dole for this important post. As majority leader, Senator Dole was responsible for getting the Senate to approve bills that President Reagan wanted passed.

Despite their political strength, the Doles were not a typical "power couple." They did not spend a great deal of time on the Washington social scene. They lived for many years in the same apartment that Bob Dole had used when he was single. In 2000, they bought the apartment next door, expanding their living space. They often ate take-out food when they finally stopped working for the night. Many friends expected that they often talked about politics when they were together at the end of the day. Some people tried to urge one to influence the other to back a favored idea. In truth, they spent very little time talking about issues. Days were often long, hectic, and full of demands. At night, they simply liked to relax and enjoy each other's company.

They also enjoyed the friendship of a new pet. In late 1984, Elizabeth gave Bob a pet schnauzer. The gift was given in honor of Bob Dole's becoming majority leader, making the dog's name an easy choice—"Leader." Leader lived with them for 15 years until he died in 1999. In the last few years of the pet's life, Elizabeth or Bob often took him to the work with them. About a year after Leader's death, a dog that was Leader's grandson came into their lives.

Sometimes the Doles had wildly different schedules. When one had to leave home early for a meeting or interview, the other might still be asleep. When that happened, the one leaving home first often left a note for the sleeping spouse. Of course, their travel schedules frequently forced the Doles to be apart. Whenever one or the other was on the road, they spoke often on the telephone. Sometimes, the demands of travel forced them to spend special times apart. One year, on their wedding anniversary, Bob had to be in Washington while

MAJORITY AND MINORITY

The political party with the most senators is called the majority. Members of this party act as the chairs, or heads, of each committee that oversees specific areas of law. The party with fewer seats is called the minority. Both the majority and minority parties choose a leader, who directs that party's activities in the Senate.

The majority leader has several important jobs. He or she sets the Senate schedule. That is, the majority leader decides when a bill is ready to come to a vote. If the leader backs a bill, he or she will wait until there are enough senators to vote in favor of the bill. If the majority leader disapproves of a bill, he or she might bring it to an early vote, before it has enough votes to pass.

The majority leader does not act completely alone. He or she typically works the Senate schedule out with the minority leader. The two also agree on rules for debate on a bill and other procedural issues.

Sometimes, the two leaders clash. The majority party, which has the most votes, often wins these disagreements. That outcome is not certain, though. The majority leader cannot simply ram a piece of legislation through the Senate. Senate rules allow any senator to speak for an unlimited amount of time on any issue. Senators can use this right to "filibuster"—to stop any bill they do not like from coming to a vote. A majority can block a filibuster and force a vote. For that move to work, however, the Senate needs an extra large majority. There are 100 Senators, but ending debate requires 60 (not just 51) of the senatorial votes.

Elizabeth was in Iowa. He arranged for eight friends to join her at dinner and for flowers to be delivered at the restaurant where they were dining. She arranged to have a meal from one of his favorite restaurants delivered to his Senate office. That night, they talked on the phone.

The Doles never had any children. Elizabeth was nearly 40 when they married, and Bob was in his middle 50s. While that is older than most people typically start a family, they could have decided to have children. Other older couples have made that choice. But they never did. Elizabeth once explained the reason that they had no children to an interviewer. "We realized that we were, this was, in terms of our ages, a late marriage in terms of having children. And our feeling was if that does not happen, uh, we have so many opportunities to make a difference for a lot of children."[73] Another reporter asked her mother if she thought Elizabeth ever regretted not having children. Her mother responded quickly and with certainty. "I don't think she grieves about that at all," she said.[74]

While she was happily married and happy in her work, Elizabeth Dole felt something was missing from her life. Religion had been important to her early in life. In the early 1980s, though, she came to see that work was crowding out her faith. "Sunday," she explained in her autobiography, "had become just another day of the week. . . . Though I was blessed with a beautiful marriage and a challenging career, my life was close to spiritual starvation."[75] As she thought about this, she reflected on the very different spiritual example that her grandmother Mom Cathey had set.

In response to these feelings, Elizabeth Dole joined a small group of like-minded people and began to attend their meetings. They met in a church, coming together once a week to talk about what God meant to them and how to bring religion into their lives. They examined their own lives to try to see what was driving them. Elizabeth confronted her desire to have control over her life. She saw that her perfectionism was leading her to make work the sole focus of her life. In an interview, she explained how she wanted to change. "I knew it was time to cease living life backwards, time to strive to put Christ first—with no competition—at the very center of my life. It was time to submit my resignation as master of my own little universe."[76]

Through this experience, Elizabeth Dole felt a spiritual rebirth. She and Bob began to dedicate their Sundays to the church, each other, and their friends. No more would Sunday be a workday like any other. They also adopted a new way of celebrating their birthdays, one that focused on the needs of others. Instead of receiving presents, they gave them to homeless people who were part of a church-formed group called Sarah's Circle. They also began giving money to the same charity.

Yet politics was always a presence in their lives. Mari Maseng Will, a close friend of Elizabeth's, described her as "not a political person" but a "public servant."[77] Bob Dole, in contrast, after many years of running for and holding elective office, was very clearly a politician. But politics was an important part of Elizabeth's life, too. In 1984, Bob was speaking at a Washington dinner well attended by politicians and reporters. He told the crowd that "under no circumstances would Dole be a candidate" for president that year. The crowd immediately erupted in laughter when Elizabeth loudly added, "Speak for yourself, sweetheart."[78]

In 1983, Elizabeth Dole changed jobs again, though not by running for office. Early that year, President Reagan asked her to join his administration as head of the Department of Transportation. This was a significant move. Interestingly, she did not go to political advisors to talk the appointment over. She asked the people in her evening church group what they thought. She did not have to ask Bob what he thought. They had already discussed the possibility of her getting a cabinet appointment, and he had advised her to accept such an offer if it were made.

She took the job and served as secretary of transportation

for about five years. During that time, she accomplished many things. One of her first achievements was to restore Washington's Union Station. This train station was in very poor shape until she launched its revival. She also led the department to cut down on regulations in the trucking and railroad industries.

An important step was to turn Conrail from a government company to a privately owned one. Conrail, a railroad, carried freight along the East Coast. It had been formed in the 1970s when several private railroad companies went out of business. The idea had been to revive the railroad under government control and then turn it back into a privately owned company again.

Secretary Dole first put together a deal to have another railroad company buy Conrail, but this agreement needed Congressional approval. That turned out to be difficult. For many months, she was unable to get the Senate to vote on the deal. Majority Leader Dole did not want to push the issue, fearing that others would consider it a matter of favoritism. He finally brought it to a vote, though, and the Senate narrowly approved the sale. Then Democrats in the House held the agreement up. Finally, after long delays, the other railroad company withdrew its offer to buy Conrail. Secretary Dole fell back on another other solution, offering stock in Conrail to the public. Thus, in 1987, 60 million shares of Conrail stock were sold to the public, bringing $1.9 billion into the federal government.

The federal government also owned two Washington-area airports, Dulles International and National (now Reagan National). Secretary Dole did not see why the government should have airports, especially since both badly needed money for improvements that Congress was unwilling to pay for. She put in motion plans to sell them both. She hoped to form a regional group with members from state and local governments to run the airports. As a first step, she formed a commission of government leaders to plan the transfer. Her instructions to them were blunt. "Don't tell me whether to transfer these airports. Tell me how."[79] It was a long struggle that took three years. In the end, though, the regional bodies were formed, and Congress approved the plans in 1986.

A major focus of Elizabeth Dole's work in the Department of Transportation was safety. She tackled this matter despite advice from someone experienced with transportation issues. Safety, that person said, will never generate any great interest. But Elizabeth Dole did not see the issue the same way. "I could think of no greater satisfaction," she writes, "than knowing that my efforts might contribute to the saving of lives."[80] An early step was to back the idea of adding an eye-level brake light to the rear windows of cars. The brake lights had been tested. Studies showed that the lights were inexpensive—only about $20 per car—and that they could prevent tens of thousands of accidents. That was enough to convince Dole, and she ordered carmakers to being installing the lights.

The question of air bags and automatic safety belts was a more difficult one. A rule requiring air bags in cars had been written back in the 1970s. Carmakers, though, had sued to block the rule. The Supreme Court, hearing the case, had ruled that the Department of Transportation should require air bags unless it could give a good reason not to. Dole worried that air bags would be expensive. She also believed that evidence showed that using seatbelts was a far more effective way of preventing injuries in car accidents.

Her solution was a compromise. She approved a plan that urged the states to pass laws requiring drivers and passengers to wear seatbelts. If two-thirds of the people in the country were not covered by these laws by 1986, air bags or automatic safety belts would be required in a percentage of new cars. Each year people were not covered by seatbelt laws, the percentage of new cars with air bags would increase. By 1990, automakers would be required to have these safety measures in all cars. Some critics said she should have made a stronger stand in favor of air bags. Benjamin Kelley of the Insurance Institute said, "She did not do the strong thing. She did the politically astute thing." But Dole argues that her policy was a success. The vast majority of states passed laws requiring people to wear safety belts. At the same time, automakers began putting air bags and automatic safety belts in more and more cars.

Dole's third auto-safety issue was drunken driving. Her interest in this issue had a personal edge—one of her uncles had been killed by a drunken driver. She added her voice to growing calls for raising the minimum age for drinking alcohol. She saw this as a way of cutting down on the number of teen drunken drivers and thereby of saving lives. Eventually, all fifty states passed laws that made twenty-one the legal age for drinking alcohol. Her work earned her a humanitarian award from the National Commission against Drunk Driving. The National Safety Council also gave her its Distinguished Service to Safety award.

Use of alcohol or drugs was the focus of another decision Dole made as secretary of transportation. In 1987, an Amtrak train derailed, causing a terrible accident that killed 16 people. The engineer and brakeman on the train were found to have traces of drugs in their bloodstream. Dole used the accident to push through a rule that required many department employees to take drug tests. If a test was positive, it would have to be confirmed with another test. If the second test was also positive, the employee would have to undergo treatment for drug abuse. She also took several steps to improve air safety.

Finally, Dole moved to bring more women into the Department of Transportation. She found that fewer than

20 percent of the department employees were women, about the same proportion as had been employed in the 1960s. She put in place programs to try to recruit more women. By the time she left her cabinet post, a greater share of the department employees were female.

Labor Secretary and Red Cross Champion

1987–1996

> But we're not apart from America. We are America. Our assistance is not delivered by strangers, but by neighbors. . . . We are proud professionals, volunteers and donors united by a common goal—to touch people's lives with compassion, when Nature and chance have conspired against them.
> —Elizabeth Dole, Speech to American Red Cross employees, 1999

Another presidential election loomed ahead in 1988. Ronald Reagan was finishing his second term as president and could not, by law, run again. As a result, the Republican nomination for president was up for grabs. Reagan's vice president, George Bush, was running. Bob Dole decided to try for the nomination as well. Elizabeth resigned from her post in the Department of Transportation to join his campaign.

Once again, she had given up her career to help her husband politically. This time, though, she left a high-level office as

When Bob Dole began campaigning for the Republican presidential nomination in 1987, Elizabeth resigned from her position at the Department of Transportation to support him. Some criticized her, saying that her action sent the message that a wife's career was less important than her husband's. Elizabeth defended her position, however, emphasizing that her decision was a result of choice, not obligation.

a cabinet secretary. Some people criticized her choice. These critics believed she was sending the message that a wife's career was less important than a husband's. Dole saw it as a matter of freedom of choice. She explained her reasoning in her memoir:

> The decision was mine and mine alone, and I made the decision that was right for me. . . . Not because I *had* to, but because I *wanted* to. And isn't that what we women have fought for all these years—the right to make our own decisions about our careers and our families?[81]

Still, the decision was probably not as easy as she seems to suggest in her book. For many months, she had maintained that she could keep her job and campaign for her husband. At one point, Bob Dole said in an interview that she would have to resign sooner or later. That comment caused some bad feelings on her part. "I've rarely seen her angry," a close friend told a reporter, "but she was annoyed."[82]

The Dole campaign enjoyed an early success in Iowa, where the senator won a vote among party members. Vice President Bush finished a distant third. Soon after, though, the Dole campaign stumbled in New Hampshire, where Bush won the party primary. Dole won two more primaries in the Midwest, but in early March 1988, Bush defeated him in seventeen other states. That day made it clear that the party preferred the vice president as its candidate, and the senator dropped out of the race.

Both Doles campaigned hard for Bush to win the presidency. After the election, which George Bush won, Elizabeth rested for a while and wondered what work to do next. She began thinking about starting up a group to urge Americans to give more time and money to charities. Before she had made up her mind what to do, she received a phone call. President-elect Bush wanted her to join his cabinet as secretary of labor.

The Department of Labor oversees federal laws about workers and employers. These laws cover such issues as working hours and the minimum wage—the lowest hourly amount that a worker can be paid. The laws also regulate safety in the workplace and worker training. For many years, women and members of minority groups were treated unfairly by companies when they hired workers, set salaries, or made decisions about promotions. The department now makes sure that people do not suffer discrimination on the job. Finally, the labor department has a unit that keeps track of statistics about jobs, wages, and related matters. These statistics are used to help track the country's economy.

Elizabeth Dole was not sure whether she wanted this job. She had just spent nearly five years in another cabinet position.

Perhaps, too, she felt that the labor department was a bit of a step down. That department had far fewer employees than the transportation department. Still, its policies affect most American workers and businesses. In the end, she took the job, and in 1989 she became secretary of labor.

Dole's main focus was to improve worker training. In the 1980s, jobs were becoming increasingly complex. New technologies demanded that workers learn new skills. Many young people entering the work force were not prepared for these jobs because the nation's schools were not teaching them the skills they needed. At the same time, many workers in older industries were losing their jobs. Companies were moving their factories to other countries, where workers could be paid less. Some were replacing workers with machines that could do tasks more quickly. These workers had been trained in their jobs years before. The skills they had learned for those jobs did not fit the new set of skills they needed. Dole highlighted these problems in a report her office issued in 1989. As she said, "Simply put, America's workforce is in a state of unreadiness . . . unready for new jobs, unready for the new realities, unready for the new challenges of the '90s."[83]

In her report, Dole set up a panel called the Secretary's Commission on Achieving Necessary Skills (SCANS). She gave this SCANS Commission the job of identifying what skills workers needed to have so they could succeed in the economy's new jobs. She wanted the commission members to work with business leaders and teachers to identify these basic skills. Then, she hoped, the nation's schools would begin to teach them. The Commission made its report. Soon after, schools across the country began to develop new programs to teach the needed skills.

Secretary Dole also made changes to an existing job-training program. Congress had passed the Job Training Partnership Act earlier in the 1980s. Under this act, the federal government gave money to towns and cities to set up programs to train workers for new jobs. Dole wanted to make sure that job training was directed at people who needed it the most. She changed the program to focus on people with the fewest job skills and people with disadvantages that were most difficult to overcome. The target groups included those who lacked basic skills, the homeless, and teenage mothers.

Dole also turned her attention to workplace safety. During the 1970s and early 1980s, more and more workers complained of physical problems resulting from their work. Many suffered injuries to their muscles or nerves as a result of moving the same way over and over again. This set of problems was called "repetitive motion injuries." Dole, like most Republicans, generally opposed rules that put limits on businesses. In this case, though, she felt some rules were needed because ordinary people were suffering needlessly from these injuries. "We must do our utmost to protect workers from these hazards," she said in a 1990 press release.[84] Under her direction, the department put out a set of regulations aimed at cutting down on these injuries. This plan, however, was turned down by President Bush.

More often, Dole agreed with the president's wish to limit government regulation of business. She even held back on regulations for a favorite cause of hers, increasing the number of job opportunities available to women and minorities. She asked for a study of what is called the "glass ceiling" in American companies. This is the invisible barrier that prevents women and members of minority groups from getting high-level jobs. The study produced startling results. Less than 10 percent of the people in the nation's 4,500 top management jobs were women or members of minority groups. The finding upset Dole, but she refused to back ideas that would push companies to set quotas for hiring and promoting women and minorities to these jobs. She did make many speeches on the subject, however, urging businesses to improve their record.

When it came to her own actions, Elizabeth Dole was squarely against discrimination. In her autobiography, she pointed out proudly that almost two-thirds of her top advisors were women or members of minority groups.

Critics complain about other ideas that Dole promoted as secretary of labor. Many people—especially Democrats—supported a bill moving through Congress called the Family and Medical Leave Act. This bill was meant to help workers when a family member had a medical emergency that required care by another person. The bill required companies to allow workers to leave work for a certain number of weeks without losing their jobs. During this unpaid leave, they could care for an ailing family member. Democrats pushed the bill through Congress, but President Bush opposed it. He feared that the law would hurt businesses. Secretary Dole supported his position and urged Republicans in Congress not to vote for the bill. When the president vetoed it—which meant that the bill did not become law—she approved.

Dole was also criticized for backing a change in the minimum-wage law. She wanted to create two levels for the minimum wage. One would apply to adult workers. The other, a lower amount, would be for teens. Many businesses that hired large numbers of teens, such as fast-food restaurants, backed this idea. The lower minimum wage would cut their costs. Dole argued that having a lower minimum would ensure that more teens got jobs; if the minimum were higher, businesses would simply hire fewer people. Still, many workers' groups wanted only one level of minimum wage. In the end, Congress did not go along with two-level plan.

One of Dole's biggest successes as secretary of labor was to help settle a bitter coal miners' strike. The strike had begun early in 1989 and was still dragging on by the fall. In October, Dole met with the president of the company and the head of the miners' union. She insisted that the three of them meet in private, so that the issues could be discussed with no aides or lawyers present. She hoped in this way to avoid the confrontations that often arise; she wanted to get the two sides to work together. As the three of them lunched, she got them to agree to discuss the issues with a mediator. This is a person who tries to help two parties reach an agreement in a dispute. For the mediator, Dole brought in William Usery, a former secretary of labor, who was highly skilled at such negotiations.

Usery worked closely with the two sides for many weeks. He kept in touch with Dole about progress toward a deal. Toward the end of the year, the two sides seemed to be nearing an agreement. Dole had planned to spend the Christmas holiday in Florida with her husband Bob. With a deal near, she dropped the plans and stayed in her Washington office hoping to hear news of a breakthrough. On December 31, 1989, Usery's phone call finally came. The strike was settled. The whole episode showed Dole's approach to governing—cooperation, not confrontation.

The following summer, Dole received a phone call with a new job offer. The call came from a woman who served on the board of governors of the American Red Cross. She explained that the Red Cross had been searching for a year for a new president without success. The board of governors wanted Dole for the job and wondered if she would be interested. Dole was thrilled. She viewed the offer as an "opportunity to devote all my time to an organization whose exclusive mission is to help society's victims."[85] Still, she was cautious. She later told a reporter for *Time* magazine that she "had a couple of people go in ahead of me and look at what the challenges were going to be."[86] She was satisfied with what they told her. She decided to take the job.

On February 1, 1991, Elizabeth Dole began her work

as president of the Red Cross. In her autobiography, she explained what she thinks the organization means to people:

> People trust the Red Cross to always be there when needed, and to do what is right. From my standpoint, this tradition of trust was—and is—the organization's most valuable asset. To protect and strengthen this tradition would be my overriding goal as president.[87]

Dole also pledged to not accept her salary as president in the first year. She took this step, she said, to demonstrate how

THE RED CROSS

The Red Cross is an international organization that helps people. It has many different services. When a natural disaster strikes, the organization provides relief supplies such as food, clothing, and shelter. In wartime, the Red Cross cares for the wounded and makes sure that soldiers held as prisoners are properly cared for. It also helps civilians who have lost their homes. The Red Cross also runs courses in first aid and preventing accidents. Finally, it collects blood from people willing to donate it. That blood is given to hospitals and used for people injured in accidents or having surgery.

The organization was started in Europe in 1863. At first, it worked to help soldiers wounded in wars. In 1881, a woman named Clara Barton, who had worked as a nurse during the Civil War, led the effort to organize the American Red Cross. Barton served as president of the American Red Cross for more than twenty years. She pushed the organization into new areas of work, including disaster relief.

Today the American Red Cross is one of the world's largest charity organizations. It has a yearly budget of $2.1 billion and more than 23,000 workers. In addition, it draws on the efforts of about 1.2 million volunteers.

Dole became president of the American Red Cross in 1991. Under Dole's direction, the Red Cross made enormous improvements in the quality of their blood supply and resolved their budget problems. Dole later said that her years with the Red Cross were the most fulfilling of her career.

important the group's volunteers were. She would work as a volunteer, too.

Some skeptics have commented that this act was not much of a sacrifice for Dole. She earned hundreds of thousands of dollars making speeches to various groups across the country. Still, she was giving up a salary of $200,000, which is a substantial sum of money. In addition, she had promised that most of her speaking fees would be given to charities. After subtracting taxes and making a contribution to her retirement fund, she would give the rest to worthy causes. Some critics complain that from 1991 to 1994, less than half of the $875,000 that Dole earned in speaking fees ended up donated to charities. One critical story points out that more than a quarter of the fees went into her retirement fund and that the couple kept nearly $150,000 for themselves. A newspaper story that cited similar numbers prompted Dole to send another $75,000 to charities. As a result, she gave nearly $500,000 of the $875,000 she had received in fees from those four years to charity.

As Red Cross president, Dole set a major goal: to improve the group's control of its blood supply. In the 1980s, hearings in Congress and news reports had revealed that all Red Cross blood was not safe. Some carried infections, including the virus that causes AIDS. Despite the bad publicity, the Red Cross had not solved the problem. This was important, because the Red Cross handled about half the blood used in hospitals.

Dole set out to tackle this important issue. She launched a huge project to completely revamp the way the Red Cross handled, tested, and tracked blood. Under this plan, nearly sixty labs conducting tests with outdated equipment were replaced. In their stead, the Red Cross used nine labs that had more up-to-date facilities. The plan also threw out the old method for tracking blood, which was slowed by using 28 different computer systems. In its place, the Red Cross would have a single computerized system would serve the entire organization.

In her autobiography, Dole noted these changes with great satisfaction. Not all observers agreed that she deserved credit for them, however. Writer Judith Reitman wrote a lengthy study of the Red Cross under Elizabeth Dole's direction. She said that Dole took over an organization that was on the brink of being seriously reprimanded by Congress. Dole, she said, promised Congress to make changes, but then for two and a half years, the Red Cross did nothing. Finally, Reitman said, the Food and Drug Administration

(FDA) got a court order that compelled the Red Cross to change. "It's not that she made these changes," Reitman told a reporter. "She was forced."[88]

Dole has dismissed these criticisms as unjust. The FDA did go to court, she granted, but only because it wanted the reforms that she had already put in place to happen more quickly.

Others have disagreed with Reitman's view, backing Dole. David Kessler, the head of the FDA in 1993, the year the agency took the Red Cross to court, said, "The problems . . . were not Mrs. Dole's doing. They go back years before she ever got to the American Red Cross. . . . She did everything humanly possible—and then some—to try to move that organization. . . . She deserves enormous credit."[89] Donna Shalala, who headed the Department of Health and Human Services under President Bill Clinton in the 1990s, apparently agreed with Kessler. In 1995, she testified before a committee of Congress about the Red Cross. Her testimony was very favorable:

> I can't say enough good about what the Red Cross has done. They've made a huge investment in improving the quality of their oversight and of the blood supply. And it's been particularly Mrs. Dole's leadership. She's been very tough minded about raising the standards.[90]

In the end, the Red Cross did make massive changes in its system for collecting, testing, and tracking blood. Those changes were made while Dole was president of the group and had been launched by her before any court order. Thus, it seems that she deserves some credit for the reforms.

Dole also launched a strong campaign to raise money for the organization, which was having financial difficulties when she took over. Her campaign managed to raise nearly $3.5 billion, solving the group's budget crisis. Dole proudly highlighted the fact that more than 90 percent of that money went to programs, not to administrative costs.

But her financial management of the Red Cross was also criticized. Critics had two key complaints about how the organization used the money it collected. First, the Red Cross did not quickly turn over all the money donated to meet a particular disaster. After floods in the Midwest in 1997, the Red Cross collected more than $16 million in donations. A year later, more than a quarter of the money still had not been given to flood victims. Supporters of this practice, like Dole, said it made sense. Some of the needs that people have for money are not obvious immediately after a disaster, they say. Some of that flood relief money was given to people who needed it in the year after the flood.

The second criticism addressed where Red Cross money was used. Typically when a major disaster struck, the Red Cross issued appeals for money to provide relief to its victims. People across the country then responded with donations. But the Red Cross did not use all of that money for that major disaster. Critics claimed that the Red Cross seemed to be tricking people out of their money. In an interview, Dole explained that the organization needed to hold some money in reserve. Some disasters, she said, "are smaller disasters that don't garner any press attention. And therefore, no one knows, [and as a result] no one gives." In addition, she said, "You've got to have a disaster-relief fund that is providing for these emergencies that are inevitably going to come up where money can't be raised immediately, and you have to be prepared."[91]

Being prepared was certainly important for the Red Cross during the years of Dole's presidency. In that time, the organization had to deal with several highly destructive hurricanes, earthquakes, fires, and floods. Dole traveled to many disaster sites to help comfort the people who had been hurt or made homeless or who had lost loved ones.

The experiences touched her deeply. She also traveled to some foreign countries where international relief efforts were underway. When she became president of the American Red Cross, her mother had told her how important being a Red Cross volunteer had been to her. "Nothing I ever did made me feel so important," she had said.[92] In recounting this in her autobiography, Dole seconded the idea, writing, "I had found a job that filled me with a sense of mission."[93] She repeated this idea years later, when she left the Red Cross. She told her coworkers, "The years I've spent at the Red Cross, with you, have been the most fulfilling of my career."[94]

In 1996, she once again faced the decision of what to do while her husband ran for president. Once more, she chose to leave her position to help him campaign. This time, she did not resign but took a leave of absence. She intended to return to the Red Cross after the election. Even if her husband won the presidency, she would keep her job at the Red Cross. If that happened, Elizabeth Dole would become the first First Lady in the nation's history to have a job besides that of First Lady.

The coming election marked Bob Dole's fourth attempt to win the presidency or vice presidency. This time, he got further than ever before. In the summer of 1996, the Republican Party nominated him as its candidate for president. Elizabeth Dole became a political star at the convention that named him. One night, she gave a 20-minute speech about her husband's life and character. In a remarkable performance, Elizabeth left the speaker's platform and walked among the crowd. Using a portable microphone, she spoke from the heart about the man she called "the strongest, the most compassionate and tender person" she's ever known.[95] The audience responded with great enthusiasm to her speech and her down-home delivery. Political analysts raved about her as well.

Throughout the year, Elizabeth Dole campaigned across the country for her husband. While his campaign strategy stumbled, her speeches were very effective, leading some political observers to say that the wrong Dole was running. Despite her efforts and strong support for her husband, Bill Clinton was reelected as president. Ironically, it was now Mr. Dole, not Mrs. Dole, who was without a job after the election. Elizabeth returned to the Red Cross. Bob had resigned from the Senate to focus full-time attention on his campaign. Thus, after the election, he could not return to his old Senate seat.

History Maker

1996–2003

> The United States of America deserves a government worthy of its people.
> —Elizabeth Dole, on her motivation for
> seeking the presidential nomination, 1999

> All my life I've been accustomed to challenging the odds.
> —Elizabeth Dole, resignation speech, 1999

The 1996 election had ended in defeat and disappointment for Bob Dole. For Elizabeth Dole, though, it signaled a new opportunity. She had become a rising star in the Republican Party. As the year ended, she was sixty years old, which meant that she still had the energy to take part in a grueling campaign. She had extensive experience in government. Her work as president of the Red Cross added to her qualifications. She was in charge of a huge and important national organization, allowing her to show that she could lead and manage effectively. That job also gave her a chance to travel across the country and make friends with community leaders and volunteers in many states. Being president of the Red Cross gave her another advantage. Each disaster gave her a chance to look both sympathetic and competent as she traveled to the site to comfort the hurt and lead relief efforts.

As she looked ahead, Elizabeth Dole's prospects seemed bright, and there was an important prize visible in the distance. The year 2000 would see a new presidential election, and the race would be wide open. President Bill Clinton would be finishing his second and final term, forcing Democrats to name a new candidate. That was likely to be Vice President Al Gore. But scandals had marred the end of the Clinton presidency, and it was widely believed that Gore might lose some support by being associated with the tainted president. In addition, Republicans across the country were energized by the chance to reclaim the presidency after eight years of a Democrat in the White House. Many top-level Republicans were thinking about making a bid to be the party's candidate, but no one person seemed to be a shoo-in. Elizabeth Dole was certainly in a good position to make a run for the nomination herself.

She had seen four presidential campaigns up close. She knew that a candidate needed a strong message that appealed to voters, a good organization to pull together support and win primaries, and the ability to raise lots of money to pay for advertisements and a skilled campaign staff. She knew how much work, effort, and energy were required to run for the nation's highest office. She would need time to decide if she was ready to take on that daunting challenge. First, though, Elizabeth Dole had to carry on her work at the Red Cross.

One action the Red Cross took in the late 1990s was to unveil a new system for members of the armed forces and their families to send messages to each other. For many years, the Red Cross had played an important role in transmitting news between service people and their loved ones. Messages announced the birth of a new child, the illness of a parent, or the need for a soldier or sailor to talk to a spouse about family problems. The organization passed along nearly one and a half million messages each day. Under the old system, though, service people had to find which one of nearly 150 different stations they should contact. The new system cut that confusion by creating two emergency communication centers. Service members or their families could access either center by using a special telephone number. Then the Red Cross could quickly and easily pass the message on to the person it was meant for.

After she returned to her position as Red Cross president, Dole also led the organization in its regular work of helping people out with relief aid in emergencies. There was plenty of need for that work. At one point in 1998, the Red Cross had to provide relief to the victims of 14 different disasters at the same time. While Dole focused on making sure her organization helped people, she did not forget the impact of a disaster on the innocent people who suffered. "It breaks your heart to see this," she said after visiting the destruction caused by Florida tornadoes. Still, she conveyed hope to those victims. As she told a group of tornado victims, "The force of Mother Nature will never be as strong as the force of human beings coming together."[96]

By early 1999, Elizabeth Dole was close to a decision and took the first step. On January 5, 1999, she announced that she was resigning as president of the Red Cross. Saying, "I feel I've reached my goals,"[97] Dole added that it was time to step down. She did not reveal what her future plans were, but hinted that she was thinking about doing something important. In her farewell speech to Red Cross workers, she said, "I believe there may be another way for me to serve our country. . . . I believe there may be other duties yet to fulfill." Later in the speech, she said, "I will be considering new paths, and there are exciting possibilities."[98]

In that speech, Dole paid tribute to the hundreds of thousands of people who volunteer their time to carry out the Red Cross's work. She also talked about the many successes the Red Cross had enjoyed under her leadership. She pointed to the organization's better financial position, the reforms in the blood program, and the newly improved armed forces message system.

Some outsiders did not view her work at the Red Cross as favorably. The magazine *Business Week* found her Red Cross record mixed. It gave her grades of B in planning and B- in fund raising but only Cs in management skills and employee relations. The only A it awarded Dole—an A+, in fact—was in the area of public relations. In other words, the magazine found her most skilled at building an image rather than making policy. Roy Clason, who had worked with Dole at both the Department of Labor and the Red Cross, viewed her work at the Red Cross much more positively. She had set four or five goals there, he told a reporter, and "accomplished all of those objectives and more."[99]

This more favorable view was the one more widely held by the American people. A public opinion survey by the Gallup Organization in 1999 placed Elizabeth Dole as one of the three most admired women in the United States. (The other two were then-First Lady Hillary Rodham Clinton and talk-show host and media magnate Oprah Winfrey.) Polls taken by news organizations suggested that she would be a strong presidential candidate. One poll had her and Vice President Gore running virtually dead even. The highly favorable opinion of her and these strong poll results led Dole to think that she had a chance to become the first woman to be elected president of the United States. Still, she was not immediately ready to run. What she told her close advisors before leaving the Red Cross was a more cautious message. "Let's prepare, in case," she said.[100]

Dole used the next few weeks to travel the country and think about her chances. By late spring of 1999, she had made the decision to try for the presidency. She formed a committee to explore the potential of her candidacy. While that does not sound very definite, it is a routine formality. Most candidates create such exploratory committees so they can have a group officially authorized to raise campaign money.

Dole had several advantages in the race. Experience was certainly one of them, as was the widespread respect that she had won, especially in the 1996 campaign for her husband Bob. As a Republican, she could appeal to the country's many conservative voters. As a woman, she could attract more women's votes than the average male candidate.

She also had some problems that she had to overcome. To begin with, some Republicans believed that she was not conservative enough. They pointed out that she had once been a Democrat and had often taken positions in favor of government regulation of business. Furthermore, she had never run for or held political office herself. All her government jobs had been appointed positions. While she had gained a lot of valuable experience campaigning for her husband and others, she had never campaigned on her own behalf. The demands placed on a candidate are unique; the pressures put on a candidate for president are very heavy. Finally, she did not have a very well developed campaign organization, especially in Iowa or New Hampshire. These states were important because their early votes would give the first indication of which candidates Republicans favored. Wins in these states could give a candidate the strength to keep running. Losses in either or both might derail a campaign for good.

Dole began crisscrossing the country making speeches. She focused on her extensive experience in government and her work at the Red Cross, stressing that she was well prepared for the

Elizabeth Dole, having assisted her husband Bob's various attempts at the White House, brought a substantial amount of experience to her campaign for the 2000 Republican presidential nomination. Dole made speeches throughout the country emphasizing her career of public service and numerous achievements as president of the American Red Cross.

job. As she told an Iowa crowd, "In every job I've ever had, I've set eight or ten goals, and I go after [them] with the best team of people that I could put together . . . and we get it done." [101]

She took some bold stands in her campaign. In an appearance in New Hampshire in the spring, she spoke in favor of several gun-control measures. The remarks came in the wake of a tragic incident in which two students brought guns into their high school and began shooting. Thirteen people died. In spite of this tragedy, most Republican candidates stayed away from supporting any laws limiting gun ownership, because many Republican voters strongly oppose such laws. Dole, on the other hand, saw this issue as a matter of principle. It was a brave position to take; she was booed by some who heard the speech, and the applause was subdued. It also cost her some political support, too. A New Hampshire Republican leader stopped supporting Dole as a result of the speech.

But there were personal, touching victories as well. In October 1999, she returned home to Salisbury. There, she took part in the dedication of a new elementary school named for her.

As the campaign accelerated, she hoped to build enthusiastic support with her slogan, "Let's make history!" This phrase referred to the fact that a woman had never been elected president. The message worked to some extent; a high percentage of the money coming into her campaign was given by women. But Dole was hurt by her inability to turn interest in a woman candidate into energy and dedicated support. One reporter recounted how an Iowa speech failed to excite a crowd:

> At one event, some . . . hundreds of college kids waited all morning for her to get there. The event was half an hour late. They were still there. They were all keyed up. She came in and started talking about her experience as an FTC commissioner in the '70s. That's not the kind of thing that gets hearts racing.[102]

Dole's biggest problem was fundraising. Candidate George W. Bush, the governor of Texas and the son of former President George Bush, raised many millions more than she was able to raise. Without sufficient money, Dole simply could not compete. In late October 1999, she finally had to face the fact that she did not have a chance. She withdrew from the race. In her farewell speech, she cited money woes as the reason for pulling out. Governor Bush, she said, enjoyed a 75-to-1 or 80-to-1 advantage over her in terms of campaign financing. That was too much for her to overcome. "All my life I've been accustomed to challenging the odds," Dole said. This time, though, "the odds are overwhelming." After thanking the thousands of people who had given their time and money to her campaign effort, Dole elaborated on President Theodore Roosevelt's famous words about taking risks:

'Far better it is to dare mighty things, to win glorious triumphs, even though checkered by failure, than to take rank with those poor spirits who neither enjoy much nor suffer much because they live in the gray twilight that knows not victory nor defeat.' God willing, there are many arenas in which to fight, many ways to contribute. So while I may not be a candidate for the presidency in 2000, I'm a long way from the twilight.[103]

Most political analysts agreed that Dole was wise to drop out of the race. The Bush campaign's ability to raise money would be impossible to overcome. Many of the analysts probed for other reasons her campaign had failed. What had she done—or not done—as a candidate that had hurt her chances to win? Sheryl McCarthy of *Newsday* suggested that the problem was a lack of ideas. She wrote, "I personally couldn't figure out what Elizabeth Dole stood for. Like every other presidential candidate, she talked about improving education. She also supported a strong military . . . and, unlike many Republicans, supported gun control. But she never emerged with a signature message one way or another."[104]

That criticism is not entirely fair. Elizabeth Dole took solid positions on many issues, from farm policy to gun control to the drug problem. Many of her speeches had focused on changes in education, an issue of great importance to her. In her campaign appearances she had stressed her experience and the hope that her supporters could "make history" by electing the first woman president. These messages apparently did not generate enough interest among voters—or among campaign contributors. As the *Wall Street Journal's* Paul Gigot said, "She never developed a real rationale for running, other than, 'I'm the first woman candidate; let's make history.' And you have to have something other than your résumé to run on. She never found that." [105]

Of course, Dole did not give up on the life of public service that she had always been dedicated to. When George W. Bush won the Republican nomination for president in

THE CLOSEST ELECTION

The election of 2000 was the closest presidential election in American history. George W. Bush ran as the Republican candidate for president with Dick Cheney as his running mate. The Democratic candidate was then-Vice President Al Gore, who had selected Senator Joseph Lieberman of Connecticut as his running mate.

There were several surprises during election night. As the night wore on, each candidate picked up victories in more and more states. Each state win gave a candidate a certain number of electoral votes. The candidate with a majority of those votes would become president. At one point that night, it appeared that Gore had won Florida, a victory that would have made him president. As more vote totals came in, however, it became clear that Florida had voted for Bush, an outcome that gave him the needed electoral majority.

The next day, new surprises hit the newspapers. Stories about problems in the Florida voting process emerged. The Gore team wanted to recount the ballots in a few key Florida counties. They hoped the recount would give the Democrat enough votes to win the state—and thus the presidency. The two sides became locked in bitter court struggles that would decide whether the results would stand or whether there would be a recount. Finally, the U.S. Supreme Court ruled that the original election totals should stand. George W. Bush was certified as the elected president. Ironically, the Supreme Court voted 5-to-4 for this result. In the end, the closest election in history was decided by just one vote.

2000, she campaigned hard for him and for Republican candidates for Congress.

After the 2000 election, Dole continued making public speeches while she thought about what to do next. By the end of 2001, she had decided to run for the U.S. Senate. After another jaunt on the campaign trail, Dole won the election. The following January, Dole was sworn in as a senator representing the state of North Carolina. While she had lost her chance to make history as the first woman U.S. president, Dole had a historic triumph: she is the first woman from North Carolina to be elected to the United States Senate.

As the Senate organized, Dole was placed on four key committees. One was the Armed Services Committee, the unit that oversees the army, navy, air force, and marines. Dole wanted this appointment very much because many thousand troops and their families live in North Carolina. She hoped to push for a pay raise for soldiers. She also had seats on the Agriculture and Banking committees, which cover important industries in North Carolina. Finally, she was put on the Aging Committee, reflecting the fact that the elderly are an important group in her state.

Dole began her Senate career with high hopes for what she could accomplish. She vowed, as she had during the campaign, to work cooperatively with Democrats to get important things done. In an interview during the campaign, she said, "Coalition-building, working across the aisle [with people of the other party], this is my kind of style, because I like results."[106] She had a great advantage coming into her new job. She knew many senators, both from her own work in Washington over many years and from her husband's two decades in the Senate. Longtime friend Mari Maseng Will put it well. "The Senate is all about relationships, and Elizabeth Dole starts with more and better relationships than a lot of people."[107] Still, Dole herself admitted that she had a lot to learn about how the

While she did not become president of the United States, Dole nevertheless lived up to her campaign slogan "Let's Make History": in 2003, Dole became the first woman to represent the state of North Carolina in the U.S. Senate. As a senator, Dole works hard to tackle the concerns of her fellow North Carolinians, whether on committees dedicated to the armed services and the elderly, or by speaking to key interest groups, like the tobacco group she is addressing in this June 2003 photograph.

Senate worked—but she looked forward to "a very interesting education."[108]

In the beginning, realizing that she much to learn, Dole did not take a very prominent role in the Senate or in national politics. She vowed to keep her focus on the needs of North Carolina's people. As she told a reporter, she intended to work for "North Carolina first."[109] Thus, the first bill that she introduced in the Senate, in the spring of 2003, aimed to give the Lumbee Indians of North Carolina recognition by the federal government as an Indian tribe. If the bill passed, the Lumbee would be eligible for more federal aid than before.

Dole also worked on other North Carolina issues. She joined with other senators in backing a measure that would increase combat pay for members of the armed forces. This would help the families of soldiers who had been sent to fight in Iraq in the spring of 2003. She joined with others to support a bill aimed at helping tobacco farmers. She also came out in favor of steps that would make it easier for more families to buy new homes.

In these moves, Dole did not take a major leadership role but took part in efforts already begun by others. In June of 2003, however, she boldly declared herself at the forefront of an important issue. That month, she gave her first speech to the Senate. In the speech, she announced her ideas for tackling the problem of hunger. Calling hunger "the silent enemy lurking within too many American homes," Dole said, "No family . . . should have to worry about where they will find food to eat."[110] One of her ideas was to give more support to "gleaning." This is collecting and donating crops that would otherwise be destroyed because they were not sold to food banks. She also pushed for making more children eligible for free school lunches.

The push against hunger showed many aspects of Dole's character. She developed her ideas after seeing and talking to people in homeless shelters and food banks. Before making the speech, she talked to important leaders, such as the secretary of agriculture, to try to build support for her idea. The issue matched her goal of helping the people of North Carolina. Farmers would benefit from her plans, and so would the nearly one million people in the state who faced hunger every day. Her speech broke important ground—it brought new attention to an important problem that had been widely ignored. Perhaps most revealing was a comment she made in an interview about why she chose to focus on hunger. "It's something," she told a reporter, "that's just been on my heart for a long time."[111]

Chronology

1936 Elizabeth Hanford born in Salisbury, North Carolina, on July 29

1939 Family moves to 712 South Fulton Street; brother's high school class names her class mascot

1950 Graduates from eighth grade; wins school citizenship award

1954 Graduates from high school; enrolls at Duke University

1958 Graduates from Duke University with distinction; begins work at Harvard Law School library

1959 Summer courses at Oxford University; trip to Moscow; enters Harvard School of Education

1960 Earns masters from Harvard in government and teaching; summer in Washington, D.C.; travels on Johnson campaign train

1961 Works at Harvard Law library most of year; spends summer working at United Nations

1962 Works summer at United Nations; enters Harvard Law School

1965 Graduates from Harvard Law; turned down for White House fellowship

1966 Passes Washington, D.C., bar; plans conference on educating the deaf for Department of Health, Education, and Welfare

1967 Stages conference; loses HEW job; begins work as public defender in Washington, D.C.

1968 Joins White House Office of Consumer Affairs

1969 Becomes deputy director of President's Committee on Consumer Interests

1973 Becomes a commissioner of the Federal Trade Commission

1974 Named one of 200 "faces for the future" by *Time* magazine

1975   Marries Bob Dole, Kansas senator

1976   Joins Dole as he campaigns for vice president

1979   Resigns from FTC; helps Dole campaign for Republican nomination for president

1980   Joins Ronald Reagan campaign after Dole drops out of race; named as head of the White House Office of Public Liaison under Reagan

1983   Becomes secretary of transportation under Reagan

1984   Bob Dole become Senate majority leader; Doles get pet dog "Leader"

1987   Resigns from department of transportation to campaign for Bob Dole

1989   Becomes secretary of labor under George Bush

1990   Resigns as secretary of labor; becomes president of the American Red Cross

1995   Temporarily leaves Red Cross to help Bob Dole campaign for president

1996   Resumes presidency of Red Cross

1999   Resigns from Red Cross to campaign for president

2000   Ends her campaign for president

2002   Elected to U.S. Senate from North Carolina

2003   Sworn in as senator

Notes

CHAPTER 1

1 Mark Wineka, "Dole Makes Formal Launch of Senate Race at Catawba," *Salisbury Post,* February 24, 2002. <http:www.salisburypost.com/ 2002feb/022402a.htm>.

2 Bob Dole and Elizabeth Dole. *Unlimited Partners: Our American Story* (New York: Simon & Schuster, 1996), 154.

3 Erskine College. <http://www.erskine.edu/news/ dolespeech.5.15.99.html>.

4 Quoted in "Looking for Elizabeth Dole," CBS News, May 1, 2002. <http://www.cbsnews.com/stories/ 2002/05/01/politics/main507749. shtml>.

5 Quoted in "Senator Dole?," *North Carolina Political Review,* September 2002. <http://www.ncpoliticalreview.com/ 0902/dol1.htm>.

6 Quoted in "Observations," *Charlotte Observer,* November 11, 2002: 1D.

7 Quoted in Rob Christensen and Amy Gardner, "Dole Makes History," *News & Observer.* <http://www.newsobserver.com/ elections/story/1890503p-1876974c. html>.

CHAPTER 2

8 Quoted in Rose Post, "Why the Hanfords Came to Salisbury: Music and Flowers," *Salisbury Post,* March 14, 1999. <http://www.salisburypost.com/ liddy/liddydole031499_2.htm>.

9 Dole and Dole, *Unlimited Partners,* 45.

10 Ibid., 47.

11 Quoted in Jennifer Ferranti, "What Drives Elizabeth Dole?," *Christian Reader,* May/June 1999. <http://www.christianitytoday.com/ cr/9r3/9r3020.html>.

12 Quoted in Rose Post, "The Early Years," *Salisbury Post,* March 15, 1999. <http:www.salisburypost.com/liddy/ liddydole031599.htm>.

13 Quotes from Post, "Early Years," *Salisbury Post.*

14 Quoted in Richard Stengel, "Liddy Makes Perfect," *Time,* July 1, 1996.

15 Dole and Dole, *Unlimited Partners,* 46.

16 Quoted in David Von Drehle, "Dole's Campaign Role: Bridging Past, Future," *Washington Post,* October 13, 1999: A1.

17 Dole and Dole, *Unlimited Partners,* 48.

18 Quoted in "Liddy Has Been Running All Her Life," *Salisbury Post,* October 3, 1999. <http://www.salisburypost.com/ october99/100399a.htm>.

19 Quoted in Post, "Early Years," *Salisbury Post.*

20 Quoted in Von Drehle, "Dole's Campaign Role," *Washington Post.*

21 Ibid.

22 Ibid.

23 Ibid.

24 Quoted in Rose Post, "'Upper Class' and Down to Earth, Too," *Salisbury Post,* March 17, 1999. <http://www.salsiburypost.com/ liddy/liddydole031799.htm>.

25 Quoted in Dole and Dole, *Unlimited Partners,* 51.

26 Ibid., 53.

27 Ibid., 53.

28 Quoted in Post, " 'Upper Class,' " *Salisbury Post.*

29 Quoted in "Liddy Has Been Running All Her Life," *Salisbury Post.*

30 Quoted in Post, " 'Upper Class.' " *Salisbury Post.*

31 Dole and Dole, *Unlimited Partners,* 43.

32 Quoted in "Liddy Has Been Running," *Salisbury Post,* October 3, 1999. <*http://www.salisburypost.com/october99/100399a.htm*>.

33 Dole and Dole, *Unlimited Partners,* 52.

34 Ibid.

CHAPTER 3

35 Dole and Dole, *Unlimited Partners,* 77.

36 Ibid., 79.

37 Ibid., 54.

38 Personal interview.

39 Quoted in Rob Christensen, "Elizabeth Dole Series: An N.C. Belle Blazes D.C. Trail," *News & Observer.* <*http://www.newsobserver.com/elections/story/1812308p-1810731c.html*>.

40 Dole and Dole, *Unlimited Partners,* 78.

41 Ibid., 79.

42 Quoted in Post, " 'Upper Class,' " *Salisbury Post.*

43 Dole and Dole, *Unlimited Partners,* 81.

44 Von Drehle, "Dole's Campaign Role," *Washington Post.*

45 Dole and Dole, *Unlimited Partners,* 81.

46 Quoted in Rose Post, "Liddy Samples World, Decides on Law School," *Salisbury Post,* March 18, 1999. <*http://www.salisburypost.com/liddy/liddydole031899.htm*>.

47 Dole and Dole, *Unlimited Partners,* 84.

48 Ibid., 87.

49 Ibid., 89.

50 Ibid., 81.

51 Quoted in Christensen, "Elizabeth Dole Series" *News & Observer.*

52 Dole and Dole, *Unlimited Partners,* 90.

53 Quoted in Dole and Dole, *Unlimited Partners,* 90.

54 "Elizabeth Dole," *Business Woman Magazine,* <*http://www.bpwusa.org/Content/Business_Woman_Magazine/Fall1999/Dolearti.htm*>.

55 Dole and Dole, *Unlimited Partners,* 91.

56 Ibid., 94.

CHAPTER 4

57 Dole and Dole, *Unlimited Partners,* 135.

58 Exchange quoted in Dole and Dole, *Unlimited Partners,* 136.

59 Dole and Dole, *Unlimited Partners,* 138.

60 Ibid., 138.

61 Ibid., 141.

62 Quoted in Rose Post, "Tug of Washington Irresistible to Young Lawyer," *Salisbury Post,* March 19, 1999. <*http://www.salisburypost.com/liddy/liddydole021999.htm*>.

Notes

63 Dole, "Homebuyer Warranties" speech to National Association of Home-Buyers Annual Convention, Los Vegas, Nevada, January 21, 1979. <*http://www.hobb.org/dole.shtml*>.

64 Dole and Dole, *Unlimited Partners,* 155.

CHAPTER 5

65 Quoted in Christensen, "Elizabeth Dole Series," *News & Observer.*

66 Dole and Dole, *Unlimited Partners,* 163.

67 Ibid., 168.

68 Ibid., 171.

69 Ibid., 172.

70 Quoted in Dole and Dole, *Unlimited Partners,* 178.

71 Dole and Dole, *Unlimited Partners,* 185.

72 Ibid., 199.

73 Quoted in Van Dehle, "Dole's Campaign Role," *Washington Post.*

74 Quoted in "Liddy Makes Perfect," *Time.*

75 Dole and Dole, *Unlimited Partners,* 24.

76 Quoted in Ferranti, "What Drives Elizabeth Dole?" *Christian Reader.*

77 Quoted in "Liddy Makes Perfect," *Time.*

78 Quoted in Van Dehle, "Dole's Campaign Role," *Washington Post.*

79 Quoted in Dole and Dole, *Unlimited Partners,* 255.

80 Dole and Dole, *Unlimited Partners,* 223.

CHAPTER 6

81 Dole and Dole, *Unlimited Partners,* 271.

82 Quoted in Alessandra Stanley, "Secretary Dole, Meet Mrs. Dole," *Time,* September 21, 1987.

83 Quoted in City College of San Francisco SCANS web site, "The Creation of the SCANS Report." <*http://www.ccsf.edu/Services/ Vocational_Education/ove/SCANS/ history.html*>.

84 Quoted in "OSHA Hearings Will Stress Need for Workplace Ergonomics Standards," *Northwest Labor Press,* April 4, 2000. <*http://www.nwlaborpress.org/ 4-21-00OSHA.html*>.

85 Dole and Dole, *Unlimited Partners,* 283.

86 Quoted in Erik Larson, "First Blood: How the Red Cross Wounded a Resume," *Time,* July 1, 1996.

87 Dole and Dole, *Unlimited Partners,* 288–89.

88 Quoted in David Rice, "Dole's Management of the Red Cross Praised by Some, Faulted by Others," *Winston-Salem Journal,* October 27, 2002. <*http://www.journalnow.com/wsj/ specialreports/helms/doleprofile.html*>.

89 Quoted in Rice, "Dole's Management of Red Cross," *Winston-Salem Journal.*

90 Ibid.

91 Ibid.

92 Quoted in Dole and Dole, *Unlimited Partners,* 290.

93 Dole and Dole, *Unlimited Partners,* 290.

94 "Text of Liddy Dole Resignation Speech," *Salisbury Post,* January 5, 1999. <*http://www.salisburypost.com/ liddy/liddydole010599_text.htm*>.

95 Elizabeth Dole, speech to the 1996 Republican National Convention, from Gifts of Speech website. <*http://gos.sbc.edu/d/dole.html*>.

CHAPTER 7

96 Quoted in "Red Cross Pres Comforts Tornado Victims" from Disaster Relief web site <*http://www.disasterrelief.org/ Disasters/980225dole/*>.

97 Mark Wineka, "Dole Leaves Red Cross." *Salisbury Post,* January 5, 1999. <*http://www.salisburypost.com/ liddy/liddydole010599.htm*>.

98 Quoted in "Text of Dole Resig- nation Speech," *Salisbury Post.*

99 Quoted in Rose Post, "Dole Going Under the Microscope." *Salisbury Post,* March 21, 1999. <*http://www.salisburypost.com/ liddy/liddydole032199_2.htm*>.

100 Quoted in Michael Duffy, "And Now It's Her Turn," *Time,* January 18, 1999. 101. Quoted in "Dole on the Trail," Online NewsHour. <*http://www.pbs.org/newshour/bb/ election/july-dec99/dole_10-18.html*>.

102 Warner, Margaret. "Dole on the Trail." Online NewsHour. <*www.pbs.org/newshour/bb/election/ july-dec99/dole_10-18.html*>.

103 Elizabeth Dole. "Withdrawal Speech" 2000gop.com. <*http://www.2000gop.com/dole/ dolespeech.html*>.

104 Quoted in "Dole Editorial Excerpts." *Salisbury Post,* October 24, 1999. <*http://www.salisburypost.com/ october99/102499i.htm*>.

105 Quoted in Gwen Ifill, "Bowing Out." Online NewsHour. <*http://www.pbs.org/newshour/bb/ election/july-dec99/dole_10-20.html*>.

106 Interview with Elizabeth Dole, CNN.com. <*http://www.cnn.com/TRANSCRIPTS/ 0208/10/en.00.html*>.

107 Quoted in Jim Morrill and Charles Hurt, "New Senators Bring Experience" *Charlotte Observer,* November 10, 2002: 1A.

108 Quoted in Scott Mooneyham, "Dole Begins New Career in Senate." *Charlotte Observer,* January 7, 2003. <*http://www.charlotte.com/mld/ charlotte/news/breaking_news/ 4893975.htm*>.

109 Quoted in John Wagner, "Dole Keeping a Low Profile." *News & Observer,* May 5, 2003. <*http://www.newsobserver.colm/ politics/dole/story/2596529p- 2335911c.html*>.

110 Quoted in John Wagner, "Dole Tackles 'Silent Enemy.'" *News & Observer,* June 6, 2003. <*http://www.newsobserver.com/ politics/dole/story/2596529p- 2409447c.html*>.

111. Quoted in Wagner, "Dole Tackles 'Silent Enemy,'" *News & Observer.*

Bibliography

Christensen, Rob, and Amy Gardner. "Dole Makes History." *News & Observer.* *www.newsobserver.com/elections/story/1890503p-1876974c.html.*

Christensen, Rob. "Elizabeth Dole Series." *News & Observer* (March 25, 2003). *http://www.newsobserver.com/extra/story/1905006p-1810731c.html.*

City College of San Francisco. "The Creation of the SCANS Report." *www.ccsf.edu/Services/Vocational_Education/ove/SCANS/history.html.*

Crawford, Craig. "Looking for Elizabeth Dole." *CBS News* (May 1, 2002). *www.cbsnews.com/stories/2002/05/01/politics/main507749.hmtl.*

Dole, Bob, and Elizabeth Dole. *Unlimited Partners: Our American Story.* New York: Simon & Schuster, 1996.

"Dole Editorial Excerpts." *Salisbury Post* (October 24, 1999). Available online at *www.salisburypost.com/october99/102499i.htm.*

Dole, Elizabeth. "Elizabeth Dole." *Business Woman Magazine* (Fall 1999). Available online at *www.bpwusa.org/Content/Business_Woman_Magazine/Fall1999/Dolearti.htm.*

———. "Elizabeth Dole's Commencement Speech at Erskine College." *Erskine NetNews.* Available online at *www.erskine.edu/news/dolespeech.5.15.99.html.*

———. "Homebuyer Warranties" Speech. National Association of Home-Buyers Annual Convention, Las Vegas, Nev. (January 21, 1979). Text available online at *www.hobb.org/dole.shtml.*

———. "Resignation Speech." *Salisbury Post* (January 5, 1999). Available online at *www.salisburypost.com/liddy/liddydole0105099_text.htm.*

———. "Speech to the 1996 Republican National Convention." *Gifts of Speech.* Available online at *gos.sbc.edu/d/dole.html.*

———. "Withdrawal Speech." 2000gop.com. *www.2000gop.com/dole/dolespeech.html.*

Duffy, Michael. "And Now It's Her Turn." *Time* (January 18, 1999). Available through the archives online at *www.time.com.*

Ferranti, Jennifer. "What Drives Elizabeth Dole?" *Christian Reader* (May/June 1999). Available online at *www.christianitytoday.com/cr/9r3/.*

Hurt, Charles, and Jim Morrill. "New Senators Bring Experience." *Charlotte Observer* (November 10, 2002): 1A.

Ifill, Gwen. Interview with Mark Shields, "Bowing Out." Online NewsHour. *www.pbs.org/newshour/bb/election/july-dec99/dole_10-20.html.*

Larson, Eric. "First Blood: How the Red Cross Wounded a Resume." *Time* (July 1, 1996). Available through the archives of *Time* at *www.time.com.*

McNew, Jessica Gregg. "Red Cross President Comforts Tornado Victims." *Disaster Relief.* Available online at *www.disasterrelief.org/Disasters/ 980225dole/.*

Mooneyham, Scott. "Dole Begins New Career in Senate." *Charlotte Observer* (January 7, 2003). Available online at *www.charlotte.com/mld/charlotte/news/breaking_news/4893975.htm.*

"Observations." *Charlotte Observer* (November 11, 2002): 1D.

"OSHA Hearings Will Stress Need for Workplace Ergonomics Standards." *National Labor Press* (April 4, 2000). Available online at *www.nwlaborpress.org/Archives/2000/4-21-00OSHA.html.*

Post, Rose. "Dole Going Under the Microscope." *Salisbury Post* (March 21, 1999). Available online at *www.salisburypost.com/liddy/liddydole032199_2.htm.*

————. "Liddy Samples World, Decides on Law School." *Salisbury Post* (March 18, 1999). Available online at *www.salisburypost.com/liddy/ liddydole031899.htm.*

————. "Tug of Washington Irresistible to Young Lawyer." *Salisbury Post* (March 19, 1999). Available online at *www.salisburypost.com/liddy/ liddydole031999.htm.*

————. "Why the Hanfords Came to Salisbury: Music and Flowers." *Salisbury Post* (March 14, 1999). Available online at *www.salisburypost. com/liddy/liddydole031499_2.htm.*

Rice, David. "Dole's Management of the Red Cross Praised by Some, Faulted by Others." *Winston-Salem Journal* (October 27, 2002). Available online at *www.journalnow.com/wsj/specialreports/helms/ doleprofile.html.*

"Senator Dole?" *North Carolina Political Review* (September 2002). *www.ncpoliticalreview.com/elections/story/1890503p-1876974c.html.*

Stanley, Alessandra. "Secretary Dole, Meet Mrs. Dole." *Time* (September 21, 1987). Available through the archives of *Time* at *www.time.com.*

Stengel, Richard. "Liddy Makes Perfect." *Time* (July 1, 1996). Available online at *www.cnn.com/ALLPOLITICS/1996/analysis/time/9607/01/ stengel.shtml.*

Bibliography

Von Drehle, David. "Dole Campaign's Role: Bridging Past, Future." *Washington Post* (October 13, 1999).

Wagner, John. "Dole Keeping a Low Profile." *News & Observer* (June 6, 2003). Available online at *www.newsobserver.com/politics/dole/story/ 2596529p-2335911c.html.*

———. "Dole Tackles 'Silent Enemy.' " *News & Observer* (June 6, 2003). Available online at *www.newsobserver.com/politics/dole/story/ 2596529p-1409447c.html.*

Warner, Margaret. Interview with Elizabeth Dole, "Dole on the Trail." *Online NewsHour. www.pbs.org/newshour/bb/election/july-dec99/ dole_10-18.html.*

Wineka, Mark. "Dole Leaves the Red Cross." *Salisbury Post* (January 5, 1999). Available online at *www.salisburypost.com/liddy/ liddydole010599.htm.*

———. "Dole Makes Formal Launch of Senate Race at Catawba." *Salisbury Post* (February 24, 2002). Available online at *www.salisburypost.com/2002feb/022402a.htm.*

Further Reading

Books

Bonner, Mike. *How to Become an Elected Official.* Philadelphia: Chelsea House, 2000.

Dole, Bob, and Elizabeth Dole. *Unlimited Partners: Our American Story.* New York: Simon and Schuster, 1996.

Feinberg, BarbaraSilberdick. *The Cabinet.* New York: 21st Century Books, 1997.

Fish, Bruce, and Becky Durost Fish. *The History of the Democratic Party.* Philadelphia: Chelsea House, 2000.

Hakim, Joy. *All the People. Vol. 2 (A History of Us).* New York: Oxford University Press Children's Books, 1995.

Jones, Veda Boyd. *The Senate.* Philadelphia: Chelsea House, 2000.

Lutz, Norma Jean. *The History of the Republican Party.* Philadelphia: Chelsea House, 2000.

Sobel, Syl. *How the U.S. Government Works.* New York: Barrons, 1999.

Websites
Elizabeth Dole

http://senate.dole.gov
Official Senate website

Salisbury Post

http://www.salisburypost.com/liddy/liddy_indx.htm
Archive of articles from 1998–2001 at the "Liddy Dole Index"

http://www.salisburypost.townnews.com/special_reports/liddy_watch
Archive of current articles at the "Liddy Watch Index"

Christianity Today

http://www.christianitytoday.com/cr/9r3/9r3020.html
An article about Dole's spiritual life, including an interview with her

Index

Index

Credits

About the Author

Dale Anderson studied English and American literature at Harvard University. He has worked in publishing ever since. He lives with his wife and two sons in Newtown, Pennsylvania, where he writes and edits textbooks and nonfiction books. He has written many books for young adults on history, including biographies of Saddam Hussein, Maria Mitchell, and William Wordsworth.